Tocqueville

Tocqueville

Hugh Brogan

Collins/Fontana

First published in Fontana 1973
Copyright © Hugh Brogan 1973

Printed in Great Britain
by Richard Clay (The Chaucer Press) Ltd.,
Bungay, Suffolk.

Contents

Preface

This little book cannot and does not pretend to be more than a guided tour of its subject. I have tried to be brief, lucid, accurate and uncontroversial, and to include as many points as are compatible with this attempt; but my guide's patter will inevitably leave the informed impatient with my omissions. It will also, I hope, leave the uninformed interested and dissatisfied enough to seek fuller knowledge in the writings of others, especially of course in the pages of Tocqueville himself. They will quickly discover how much I have left out: above all, any consideration of Tocqueville's minor published works; of his letters, conversations and speeches; of his notebooks of travel. I can only say that I too regret these omissions, but space, or lack of it, made them inevitable.

I have to thank Professor G. W. Pierson for kind permission to use a passage from his *Tocqueville and Beaumont in America* – not to mention his great kindness to me when I began work on Tocqueville at Yale nine years ago. I must also thank Miss C B A Behrens, Dr Michael Biddiss, Mr Simon Schama and Mr Hugh Tulloch, all of whom gave me invaluable advice on numerous points. It is my fault, not theirs, if what follows is still imperfect.

H.B.

St John's College, Cambridge,
St John the Evangelist's Day, 1971.

1   The Problem of Alexis de Tocqueville

His life was a short, and not especially merry one. His output of publications was meagre. His political career miscarried, and he laboured always under the burden of severe ill-health. He was an aristocrat in a middle-class era, and his temperament, cross-grained, refined, severely intellectual, private, would have limited the impact of his personality in any age. Yet Tocqueville commanded huge influence, during his lifetime (1805–1859) and for many years after his death; and after a long eclipse he again enjoys immense attention.

The nineteenth and the twentieth centuries hailed him for different reasons. In his own day, he was successful because he spoke directly about some of that day's most pressing concerns, in immediately intelligible terms. His period of eclipse arose naturally when men's preoccupations altered. He was redis-covered when a new age came to believe that in the pages of this long-dead writer light on some urgent, recent problems could be found. A brief survey of each of these phases in turn should make plain the implications of this history of a fashion, and what the present Tocquevillean problem is.

Tocqueville owed his original success to his first book, *De la Démocratie en Amérique*, the first two volumes of which were published in 1835, when he was not quite thirty, and which made him famous almost overnight. They and he richly deserved such a reward. The *Démocratie* is, first and foremost, the best book ever written about the American political system – argu-ably the best ever written about America. Its vivid picture of transatlantic political society fascinated and enlightened its first readers, and is still indispensable to students of the United States. Secondly, Tocqueville was a pioneer sociologist. In its day, *De la Démocratie en Amérique* was a highly original work of sociology : readers were deeply impressed by its suggestive-ness, and by the model it offered of the purpose, principles and method of sociological enquiry. Since it was also written in a pellucid style, it was clearly a masterpiece; but its diversity was still unexhausted. For it was also a political testament. In its pages the liberals of the eighteen-thirties found an empirical, eloquent, in places indeed a religious defence and exposition of their principles, which was profoundly encouraging to men embattled simultaneously against old monarchies and new socialists. The mid-nineteenth century being the liberal epoch *par excellence*, it is no wonder that the *Démocratie* became a sacred book.

But at no time were the liberals and democracy to enjoy unchallenged success, least of all in France; and the failure of a political career which at one stage had seemed highly promising spurred Tocqueville to re-examine his premisses. He had been driven into political retreat by Louis Napoleon Bonaparte's *coup d'état* in 1851; and in the bitterness of an enforced retirement he asked himself what had gone wrong. The answer came in *L'Ancien Régime et la Révolution*, published in 1856. This work expressed Tocqueville's longstanding conviction that all the troubles of modern times could be traced back to the French Revolution and beyond, to the conditions which brought it about; but like the *Démocratie* it is a many-layered, indeed in a sense an ambiguous book. It had just as huge a success. This time Tocqueville's readers found a superb sociological portrayal of pre-Revolutionary French society, strictly comparable to his portrayal of democratic America; they found a pioneering work of historiography; they found, once more, an impassioned belief in freedom and France, and in freedom as the right destiny of France, which made the whole book, from one aspect, a polemic against the autocracy of Napoleon III. To complete the success, the author's literary powers had, if anything, improved with the years.

It is not surprising, then, that in the eighteen-sixties, when democracy in America was fighting for its life; when England was moving uncertainly towards the Second Reform Act; and when Napolean III was mounting the experiment of the liberal empire, Tocqueville's (posthumous) influence reached its height. After 1870 things were bound to take a sharply different turn. Tocqueville had been both a defender of élitist values against egalitarianism, and a defender of liberty. Now Napoleon III, his great adversary, had succumbed, but to the hammer-blows of Bismarck, not to the libertarian instincts of the French. The

Third Republic incarnated many of Tocqueville's political principles – it was liberal, and contained the challenge of egalitarianism – but for that very reason its general dinginess rubbed off on its prophet. Bismarck and Karl Marx between them drew the world's attention to possibilities and problems which Tocqueville had largely ignored. America wallowed in the ignobilities of the Gilded Age. Even in England, where Tocquevillism had always been most at home, his greatest follower, John Stuart Mill, apparently turned socialist. The continuing success of élitist politics and an élitist society on the one hand made any continuing preoccupation with the defence of élitism, such as Tocqueville's, unnecessary, and on the other hand made a further challenge to élitism, and so to Tocquevillism, inevitable in due course. Before long Tocqueville was a spent force. He survived as a byword for sententious pomposity on the French stage 'comme a dit M. de Tocqueville . . .' and was dismissed with faint praise, in a couple of sentences, by Gide's schoolboys in *Les Faux Monnayeurs*. By the early twentieth century, in short, it seemed that the early nineteenth century had claimed its own for ever.

Only in America were things a little better, and it was from America that the wind of revival was to blow. Tocqueville's varied achievement might be remembered for only one of its components, but it was remembered. His discussion of American democracy as a working system remained current : James Bryce, for example, found it necessary to give prolonged consideration to *De la Démocratie en Amérique* when equipping himself to write his own masterpiece, *The American Commonwealth* (1888), and Tocqueville's remained a name to conjure with in the perennial discussions of the destiny of America by jurists, professors and philosophically-minded politicians. Besides, Tocqueville, by his courteous, fair-minded, indeed in places enthusiastic depiction of American democracy – such a contrast to the philippics of Mrs Trollope and Charles Dickens – had in his time done great service to the United States. Now the favour was returned. In 1938 an American scholar, Professor George W Pierson, of Yale, revealed for the first time the wealth of insight and material contained in Tocqueville's notebooks of his journey to America; and once again, in an age of challenge to liberty and democracy, it began to seem as if the forgotten publicist said something worth hearing. The great dictatorship looked the sort of democratic aberration against which he had issued many grave warnings.

The Second World War was another stroke of luck for Tocqueville, if for nobody else. A Frenchman who wrote about America and married an English wife, he was positively a symbol of the Western alliance. Nor did it hurt him that, halfway through his *Démocratie*, he had prophesied, or was thought to have prophesied, that the world-struggle of the future would be between America and Russia. As the Cold War deepened a fancied need for a liberal counter-Marx grew strong. Tocqueville was cast for the part. Speechwriters soon discovered that his aphoristic style made him a bottomless mine of quotable quotations: 'comme disait M. de Tocqueville ...' became a catchphrase in American translation ('as that great friend of America and democracy, Alexis de Tocqueville, so wisely remarked ...'). Such was his authority that on one occasion, when it happened that for once no suitable remark could be found in his works, a suitable remark was made up for him, and used by General Eisenhower in a speech in 1952. (Sixteen years later Mr Nixon revived it for his own presidential campaign in 1968.) Anything was better than presenting yourself to the voters without a handy Tocqueville quote at your hip.

Tocqueville was also assisted by the boom in sociology. He was unquestionably a sociologist, and if he had a fault, it was a tendency to take himself too seriously. American sociologists, whom their worst friends have never found it necessary to defend against charges of frivolity, took him to their hearts; and as American political science followed along the path of solemn unintelligibility Tocqueville's writings were doubly combed for 'insights' which, rendered down into jargon and suitably garnished with diagrams and equations, could enhance the reputation and salaries of gentlemen with academic careers to make and academic families to feed. What Tocqueville, that master of lucidity, would have made of it all defies imagination.

Tocqueville's true friends regarded all this with mixed feelings. It was gratifying that Tocqueville was respected again; that money could be found for a scholarly edition of his works and papers, to be directed by Professor J P Mayer; that so many people could read him with pleasure and profit. But the uses to which the great name was put were, in many cases, highly disturbing. Scholars researching into Tocqueville rediscovered the nineteenth-century man: a man with many of the limitations of his age, a man frequently wrong, a man whose message was directed not to posterity, let alone a Cold War posterity, but to his own time; a man who, nevertheless, the historical imagination could love and respect as one wise, courageous and richly talented, from whose writings much of the highest value was still to be learned. The problem was, and is, to drive the false Tocqueville – the democratic capitalist with all the answers – from the field, and gain attention for the real man. This is the present problem of Alexis de Tocqueville; and it is as a contribution to its solution that this book is offered.

No student of Tocqueville can read him for very long without becoming aware of his personality. Even in the *Démocratie*, where he tried most conscientiously to suppress himself in the interests of his book, a process which resulted in what Acton, rather unkindly, called his 'chill sententiousness', temperament keeps breaking through. In his other works, above all in his *Souvenirs*, and of course in his letters and notebooks, the individuality is inescapable. Tocqueville's writings have the charm of personality, which ought to be remarked on and analysed, since it is so powerful a part of the work. Some biographical description is therefore essential. It must not go too far. Tocqueville was not the simple product of forces working equally upon him, and his opinions, on the whole much more important to us than his tastes, wear a notably impersonal air. They were to a large extent formed by the free operations of his intellect, and it is on their formation that we must concentrate. But even the opinions owed much to the circumstances of his life; and we must not lose sight of the tastes entirely.

For one thing, they were so entirely of a piece with his environment. It is reassuring to discover that the commentator on his times was so much at one with them. He was fond of dogs, which feels right in an aristocrat; he was a strong swimmer (though he nearly drowned, from over-confidence, in America) and a first-rate marksman (on board ship on the way over he won a shooting match, sinking the barrel thrown overboard for gentlemen to aim at). These characteristics, too, seem suitable in a man who, born in Paris, eventually received, as his share of the family inheritance, the little *château* of Tocqueville in Normandy, and there settled down as a countryman, his life slowly filling up with the problems of farming and land improvement. Gradually he came to dominate the neighbourhood: the *curé*, just like an English parson in the olden days, was bidden to dine from time to time, when no guests of importance were expected, or none who would mind such company. Under the July Monarchy and the Second Republic Tocqueville sat on the local *conseil général* (say, county council) and the neighbourhood properly chose him to represent it in the Chamber of Deputies: though he lost the first time that he stood, in 1837, soon after settling in Normandy, he won every other election from 1839 until the *coup d'état* of 1851. In 1848, during the first election under universal male suffrage, he duly shepherded all the inhabitants of his village to the polls: 'They formed themselves into a double column in alphabetical order; I preferred to take the place my name warranted, for I knew that in democratic times and countries one must allow oneself to be put at the head of the people, but must not put oneself there' (*Souv.* 114). But naturally he was constrained to make a speech, and naturally they all voted for him. Less pleasing, yet equally revealing of his inborn attitudes, was his notorious inability to like, co-operate with or even be civil to fellow Deputies who happened to be members of the middle class. Tocqueville knew it was his duty to cultivate these men, whom he aspired to influence politically; but he found them vulgar, and to exploit personal relations for political ends was something he could not bring himself to attempt. So hands went unshaken, faces went unrecognised, and the leader went unfollowed. This is the Tocqueville whom Daumier caught in a memorable caricature, smiling quizzically, perhaps even a little cynically, alert, even formidable, but (important papers tucked under one arm) clearly fidgeting to be off, and playing impatiently, characteristically, with the eyeglass that was his constant companion.

Those who penetrated a little behind the amiable but aloof arisocratic mask found a vivacious, sympathetic companion, excellent company, expert at the *douceur de vivre* of the eighteenth century. He was welcome at all the best *salons* of Paris, where the men of talent let off their conversational fireworks for the delight of cultivated, and often beautiful, ladies, inspired by nothing stronger than weak tea and biscuits. Tocqueville was pleasing to women, for not only was he naturally good company, he greatly enjoyed their society. A sure test, which he passed with flying colours, was the marriage of his friends: the wives all accepted Alexis, and made an intimate of him, as he already was of their husbands. To his own wife he was passionately devoted; but she was not his only female *con-*

fidante. There was also Mme Swetchine, for example, a Russian lady of fervent piety, to whom he opened the secrets of his religious life. And the wife of his closest friend, Gustave de Beaumont, had such a just and fervent devotion to Tocqueville that she saved for posterity an important letter to Mme Swetchine that her husband wanted to destroy.

Up to a point, it was easy to win Tocqueville's close friendship if he approved of you. He was seldom or never the first to commit himself; but if an intellectual or political correspondent – say, the Englishman Nassau Senior, or the German-American Franz Leiber – showed the slightest wish for intimacy, he immediately became the, one hopes, delighted recipient of a torrent of affectionate messages, confidences and allusions, kept up from letter to letter with a variety and constancy which guarantee the writer's sincerity. Tocqueville enjoyed the company of his family and friends, he had immense warmth of heart, and was rewarded with utter devotion. It was very Victorian of Mrs Grote, the talented but eccentric and definitely overpowering wife of the English historian, to write in 1873 on hearing of the death of John Stuart Mill

> I have during the last twenty years felt poignant sorrow through death of friends, and for four individuals above all –
>> CATHERINE STANLEY,
>> FELIX MENDELSSOHN,
>> ALEXIS DE TOCQUEVILLE,
>> J. S. MILL

but we cannot doubt her sincerity, or that Tocqueville, even though he laughed and groaned over Mrs Grote's excesses behind her back, deserved her affection.

But there was a line which few crossed, none of his English friends among them. He would talk politics, history, literature (he had a deep knowledge of the French classics of the seventeenth and eighteenth century), health, people and places with those he liked and trusted; but his deepest concerns were reserved for a handful, of whom his wife was the most important.

We have it on Acton's authority that some guest at the *château* once spoke indiscreetly of people who married beneath their rank. Tocqueville took his wife's hand and said, 'I too married beneath me; and by God! it was worth it.'

He had undoubtedly comitted a misalliance in marrying Mary Mottley. She was an anomaly in French society as it was then constituted. In her own eyes and the eyes of the English she was a lady, of the same class and education as Jane Austen. Her brothers were in the navy, her uncle (unfortunately) had done well in trade. She herself was sent in her youth to be the companion and heiress of her widowed aunt, who lived in France. In English terms she was perfectly presentable; but in the eyes of the Tocqueville family she was shockingly middle-class. Worse, she was neither rich nor a beauty; and though Alexis found her a valuable intellectual companion, that would scarcely warrant his marrying her. They opposed the match for five or six years, but Tocqueville's commitment was too deep to be resisted. He married his Mary (Marie to him) because he could not live without her, and the family had to lump it.

We should perhaps put his chronic ill-health at the root of the matter. The last and belated child of an invalid mother, he was never strong: the final decade of his life was to be spent under the threat of tuberculosis, which in the end killed him. As a young man his burning ambition and love of life enabled him to live off his nerves; but he paid the inevitable price in nervous exhaustion. He overworked and overdrove himself, and when his body took its revenge he found himself plunged into self-doubt, anxiety, all the usual penalties of such a temperament.

I shall never be happy, Marie, that is certain [he wrote, in 1834]. Nothing is in agreement within me. With a limited and incomplete capacity, I have immense desires; with delicate health, an inexpressible need of activity and emotion; with the taste for the good, passions which lead me astray; with enough intelligence to see what I ought to desire, enough folly to wish the contrary. I am of mediocre strength and mind, at the extremity in my passions and my weakness. For a man thus organized there is not the slightest chance ever, no matter what he does, of reaching a durable happiness. (G W Pierson, *Tocqueville and Beaumont in America*, p. 698)

Such plaints are common at all periods in his most intimate correspondence. They explain why he turned to Mary Mottley.

After twenty years of marriage he could still say to Mme Swetchine

> A vague restlessness and confusedly active desires have always in me amounted to a chronic malady. I am surprised only that it can attack me so strongly in circumstances where everything fosters peace of mind. I have certainly got no complaints about my God-appointed earthly lot. I have even less right than wish to call myself unhappy; and yet I lack the chief of all the conditions of happiness: a peaceful delight in present good. Yet I live beside someone whose society ought to have been enough to cure me long ago of this great and ridiculous misery; and, as a matter of fact, it has for twenty years been very good for me, giving my mind strength enough to accept my situation, though not enough to attain a habitual and complete equilibrium. My wife, whom the world knows so little, feels and thinks passionately and vehemently; she is all too capable of feeling grief acutely and responds with intense emotion to every stroke of misfortune; but she knows how to fully enjoy every good thing that comes her way. She does not torture herself over nothing; she knows how to float down tranquil days and happy times in perfect calm and restfulness. (*Correspondence*, Beaumont edition, vol. 2, p. 376)

As they grew older – she was nine years his senior – she was often ill, sometimes irritable. But the essence of their relationship is expressed in a possibly apocryphal story. Tocqueville, we are told (and can easily believe), was a rapid eater; Marie a slow one. In the early days of their marriage the husband, it is said, was once so maddened by the wife's leisurely consumption of some *pâté* that he seized her plate and threw it onto the floor. Mme de Tocqueville simply turned to the servant and asked for another helping, which, we hope, she got and enjoyed ... all married folk have their rows. The point of this one is that it illustrates perfectly the placidity in his wife which Tocqueville found so necessary, though occasionally so unendurable. She was mother, lover, nurse and companion to him : everything except the mother of his children. He earnestly wished to be a father; but without success. His tubercular condition may have made him sterile; and Marie had some chronic complaint in her womb, as well as having been forty at the time of her marriage.

So they lavished their love on their dogs, their friends and each other, and carved out a career in which Marie, her husband's prop, had an important rôle.

He could not share everything with her. Brought up, of course, as an Anglican, she had entered the Roman Catholic church before her marriage, and became extremely devout. Tocqueville, by contrast, lost his Catholic faith at the age of sixteen, when he started to read the great authors of the Enlightenment. It was an agonising experience for him, which he was never wholly reconciled to; but even on his deathbed (when he took extreme unction to please his wife) his intellect could not retract. He became a deist, retaining of his childhood faith only a passionate belief in personal immortality, which produced some odd reasoning in *De la Démocratie en Amérique*. Though his tastes remained firmly Catholic, though he continued to believe in the social utility of religion, setting his villagers a good example by going to church regularly (he set them a good democratic example too, by dismantling the lofty pew in which his lordly ancestors had been uniquely privileged to worship) he was never again a believer. He could not discuss the matter with Marie, who would merely have been distressed by it. It came as a huge relief to him to open his heart to Mme Swetchine.

His attitude to religion cut him off from more than Marie. As he himself remarked, the French Revolution had converted the French nobility from irreligion to a perception, if not of the truth, then of the social utility of Christian belief (since it might keep the lower classes quiet) (*Souv.* 121). It had also converted them from factious opposition to the Crown to devoted royalism. Tocqueville's relations were all both devout Catholics and devout royalists; and the first great crisis of his life came with the July Revolution in 1830, when he had to choose between his family traditions, indeed his family principles, and his own judgement. It is at this point that my argument begins to relate directly to the author of the books.

It may seem possible to overrate the importance of Tocqueville's aristocratic conditioning: after all, a political scientist is supposed to be rational, to be an empiricist, whose attitudes will presumably be modified, indeed determined by logic and study. In fact there can be no doubt that from first to last Tocqueville wrote as a French noble; friends commented that he was the incarnation of a *gentilhomme* of the old order, and, as we shall see, the traces of this fundamental characteristic can be found all over his writings. Indeed, his greatness was very largely the result of the struggle in the mind of this highly gifted man between his instincts and his intelligence : between his personal commitment to aristocratic values and his perception that the day of aristocracy was over for ever.

The phrase 'aristocratic values' here does not mean some vague amalgam of blood and money, garnished with snobbery. We are not here dealing with the horsocracy of England, or the selfish and corrupt court nobles of eighteenth-century Versailles, or the degenerate gentlemen of the age of Proust. Western Europe had been dominated by its aristocracy for nearly a thousand years. Now the exercise of power is seldom self-justifying for long to individuals, and never to classes. The nobles of Europe evolved a belief in the rightfulness of their power, and a code for exercising it, which was to find its most sophisticated expression in Montesquieu, but which countless earlier and later writers had expounded. It was not the base, selfish and stupid nobles who implanted such words as 'noble', 'gentle' and 'gentleman' in the ethical vocabulary of ordinary Englishmen. Tocqueville was the descendant of people who took their duties and responsibilities seriously. On his father's side he could trace his nobility back to the fifteenth century or earlier. On his mother's side he was descended from one of the great families of the *noblesse de robe*, the Le Peletiers, who had been hereditary high officials in the *parlements*, or law-courts, of the old order. Both families, the Tocquevilles and the Le Peletiers, and the families linked to them in cousinage, upheld the ancient principles. They feared God, honoured the King and served the ideal of France. Some were soldiers, some lawyers, some statesmen, like Malesherbes, Tocqueville's great-grand-father, who had protected the Encyclopaedists, acted as a re-forming minister for Louis XVI, and at length defended the King at his trial – an act for which he was guillotined. Earnest and upright, if not always very intelligent, men such as this wielded power as a class for the last time during Tocqueville's adolescence and early manhood. His father was a prefect under the Restoration, one of his elder brothers served in the expedition which captured Algiers in 1830, just before the fall of Charles X. For them the revolution of July was a terrible event. Not only did their class lose power; their ideals were once more, it seemed, as in the great Revolution of 1789, outlawed and defeated. They retired from public life.

Alexis, having been trained as a lawyer, was at the time employed as a junior magistrate at Versailles. He and his young colleague, Gustave de Beaumont, an intimate friend, could also have taken the line of least resistance, and resigned. But, with the sort of intellectual independence that had already enabled Tocqueville to throw off an outworn religious creed, they saw that the old order had irreversibly fallen, and that the attempts of Charles X and his ministers to govern as if the Revolution could be reversed had been absurd. Tocqueville wept when by chance he met the old King's carriages rolling sadly into exile along the boulevards of Versailles : they carried with them the only world in which he could feel less than exiled. But he knew that the social order was changing rapidly; that the time for old-style autocracy and aristocracy, however benevolent, was over; that henceforth the 'principles of 1789' would have the upper hand. Intelligent, upright and ambitious, Tocqueville saw no good reason for throwing away his career at its outset simply because the last Bourbon King, in his folly, had thrown away a crown. To the distress and fury of most of his family and friends, he stayed at his post.

But his position was exceedingly uncomfortable, for the new men did not really trust either him or Beaumont : promotion would be blocked, even if they were not dismissed. Some new departure was necessary. Besides, it was all very well to see that the world of liberalism had arrived. The question remained, how was it to be organised? Many of Tocqueville's aristocratic relations were convinced that it could not be organised, that in fact anarchy was impending. Were they right or wrong? Where could these matters be investigated?

The answer was, in the United States. The myth of America was at that time still waxing in potency. It was a republic, a democracy, which had succeeded where France had, hitherto, failed. Tocqueville and Beaumont decided to go to America to discover its secret. They hoped to write a book about their findings, which, sweeping them to fame, would also open a political career to them (since, though aristocratic power might be declining, the ruling élite still kept enough respect for letters to admire and support men of proved intellectual powers). As an excuse to their superiors, they proposed that they constitute themselves an official mission to investigate and report on the American prison system, which was then fermenting with interesting experiments. On the whole, the plan succeeded marvellously. The prison mission was allowed, and the resulting report was an important work of penology. Furthermore, America proved to be a forcing-house of the commissioners' talents: the outcome for Tocqueville was the first part of *De la Démocratie en Amérique*, which, as I have said, was an instant success. Beaumont's novel *Marie*, a treatment of the race question in the United States, was much less lucky; but Beaumont was to have his reward. He entered the Chamber in 1839, soon after Tocqueville, and like him was elected to the Academy of Moral and Political Sciences. In 1842 Tocqueville was elected to the Académie Française. Of less value to his prestige was appointment to the Legion of Honour, especially as Tocqueville suspected that it was an attempt to buy his support for the government of the day. By the time the Chamber met in 1840 all seemed set fair for a distinguished political career, and the second part of the *Démocratie* was on sale.

But Tocqueville was not to be a successful politician. Apart from the inability to master the art of cordiality to *bourgeois* colleagues that I have already mentioned (by contrast the genial Beaumont got on excellently with everyone) his health was too poor to make him a frequent speaker, and his reclusive, writer's habits made it impossible for him to be a great one. He improved with time, and at least one of his orations – that of 27 January 1848, in which he predicted, to a sceptical audience, the revolution that was so close at hand – was memorable by any standards; but he worked too hard at his speeches, and never acquired the happy knack of improvisation, of thinking on his feet, which is essential to parliamentary success, and which some of his otherwise much less gifted colleagues had to perfection. In a political system dominated by orators, men such as Guizot, Thiers and Lamartine, this deficiency was a serious handicap:

it prevented Tocqueville from gaining the national reputation he desired and needed.

Still, there are more ways than one of killing a cat, and more ways than one of attaining political success. The underlying reasons for Tocqueville's failure lay rather in the time than in the man.

Tocqueville was not one of those politicians who found their career on a programme, who identify themselves exclusively with a particular set of measures, or a particular nostrum for public woes (one thinks of Cobden and free trade). Rather he seems to have hoped for a career like those of, say, Sir Robert Peel and Mr Gladstone: a career spent mostly in office, where principles and programmes could evolve from the statesmanlike handling of concrete problems. In England such careers were normal. In France, under the July Monarchy, they might have been. Guizot himself could serve as a model. His long career of able administration, which began under the Restoration of 1814; his distinguished achievement as a scholar and liberal ideologist (his lectures at the Sorbonne first inspired Tocqueville with the idea of the irresistible march of equality); his oratory, his political skill, his striking gifts as a conversationalist – this was surely a valuable example, something which one might hope to emulate, something which showed what was possible.

Unfortunately what was *not* possible, by 1840, was to take this line any longer. Guizot had indulged in too many shabby parliamentary intrigues for the sake of power: he had thus forfeited Tocqueville's respect. He was drifting steadily right-wards in his political convictions – or perhaps one should say that he was being left behind by the running tide of change; and though, as we shall see, Tocqueville himself was eventually to take a conservative stance, it was always conservatism with a difference, and it was not a purblind, cynical and selfish conservatism, such as Guizot's seemed to his young, conscientiously democratic and liberal former admirer. Above all, as the forties progressed, Tocqueville began to see that Guizot, who ruled France during most of the decade, was associated with, indeed responsible for, the tendencies which were destroying the July Monarchy and, with it, all hope for a steadily, peacefully and legally evolving French political order. Tocqueville, who was a sincere democrat – for whom universal suffrage had few terrors (he had seen it work adequately in America) – who believed in honest, responsible and disinterested government – could not associate himself with a man and a party who deliberately chose to restrict the electorate to 250,000 prosperous males, and to rule by bribery and corruption. In short, Tocqueville, whose gifts and temperament marked him out for government, was forced into opposition: a process that was to continue, for rather different reasons, under the Second Republic and the Second Empire.

For the fall of Guizot and Louis Philippe in the February Revolution of 1848 brought Tocqueville and his friends not power, but only a new sort of enemy. Tocqueville was an extreme liberal in economic matters, and gladly accepted all those tenets of classical economics, such as the wage-fund idea, which reinforced his strong French respect for the rights of private property. The Revolution of 1848 was a challenge to those rights. To us it may seem most respectful, an almost timid challenge. The workers of Paris, as so often before and since, were desperate for food, shelter and work. They demanded public aid, legal recognition of the right to work and a programme of public works in which to realise that right. All this implied taxation of the propertied for the sake of the propertyless. An adumbration of the welfare state, it was too much for Tocqueville. In his eyes it was immoral, and economically impossible (on these matters he was a very *bourgeois* aristocrat). The workers who made these demands were deluded by wicked ideologues like Louis Blanc, or wicked and dangerous revolutionaries like Auguste Blanqui (had Tocqueville ever come across the *Communist Manifesto*, with its wild demands for income taxes and death duties, it would have confirmed his worst suspicions). Weaklings like Lamartine who attempted compromise, concession and conciliation was despicable. Tocqueville, and the so-called party of order to which he now adhered, wanted a showdown, and in due course got one. Driven to despair, the Parisians rose in June 1848 and were shot down to teach them sense – Tocqueville was especially gratified by the arrival of many of his Norman constituents to share in the good work. General Cavaignac, who had organised the victory, formed a new government, and Tocqueville was moving towards participation in it when the Presidential elections in December

tumbled Cavaignac from power. To Tocqueville's consterni
the mighty events of 1848 had merely opened the way
another Napoleon.

Tocqueville could never come to terms with Bonapartism.
As early as 1835 he had prophesied, in his *Démocratie*, that the
failure of democracy, of the peaceable empire of the many,
could only lead to the tyranny of a new Caesar: 'the unlimited
power of one man alone'. Though he had hoped against hope,
and worked hard for the success of the Republic, he had feared
from the first that the February Revolution was bringing about
the suppression of liberty. It was no pleasure to be proved
right. Then, Bonapartism, as interpreted by Louis Napoleon,
proved to contain many of the detested fallacies of socialism
(Louis Napoleon had been a Saint-Simonian in his youth). Its
extreme nationalism bewildered Tocqueville, because he shared
it. He had been an advocate of a forward foreign policy, and of
French colonialism in North Africa, under the July Monarchy;
if, under the Second Republic, a more prudent attitude seemed
desirable, this did not imply any fundamental change. So Tocqueville, when he became Foreign Minister for a few months
in 1849, could work quite happily with the Prince-President.
Besides, the chief problem then facing French diplomacy was
the Roman question. Louis Napoleon, like Tocqueville, wanted
to restore the Pope and yet give Rome liberal institutions (it
was one of Tocqueville's favourite notions that whenever the
Church relinquished its obsolete privileges it became infinitely
more popular, and a very useful conservative pillar of society).
But many of the Bonapartists were corrupt adventurers – greedy
as, and far more reckless than, Guizot's entourage – the Prince-
President himself was not above suspicion. Above all there
remained the awkward, indeed unforgivable fact, that at bottom Bonapartism was anti-liberal, anti-legel, authoritarian, con-
spiratorial – as was amply demonstrated by the *coup d'état* of
December, 1851, when Louis Napoleon dissolved the National
Assembly by force. This Tocqueville could never forgive. Liberty was the abiding, noblest passion of his life. After its
destruction in France he withdrew from public life to devote
himself once more to writing: to the attempt to explain to
himself and his countrymen what had gone wrong, and what
the outlook for the future might be. The pattern of modern

French history, he saw, had been largely determined by the events of the great revolution and the career of the first Napoleon; at times, indeed, it seemed as if all subsequent events were mere ridiculous repetitions, as by a third-rate rep., of the original drama. Tocqueville therefore reverted to an old interest, and embarked on a study of Napoleon I. But it quickly became apparent that Napoleon, to be understood, had to be interpreted against the background of the Revolution; and the Revolution had to be interpreted against the background of the old order. After some false starts, then, Tocqueville settled down to the study of the old order; and the result, the first volume of his projected history of the Revolution and the Empire, appeared in 1856. The work was justly acclaimed as a masterpiece, and it fundamentally altered the historiography of the subject: it was Tocqueville who first directed the attention of French historians to the provincial archives where they have since done such dazzling work. But the book was also a tract for the times: many were the pages that reflected Tocqueville's distress at the fallen state of his country, and, at the same time, his belief in her eventual resurrection. It was characteristic of the merciless tyranny of Napoleon III that the Emperor allowed this anti-Bonapartist work to appear, and to enjoy enormous success, and refrained from shooting the author.

Tocqueville, much encouraged, set to work on the second volume. But his time was running out. At first he suffered from the inevitable reaction: it was many months before his creative energy, depleted by the effort of producing the *Ancien Régime*, was renewed sufficiently to enable him to make much progress. Then there were intellectual difficulties: his *forte* was analytical, not narrative history, and for the second stage of the Revolution he had yet to discover an analytical principle – a working hypothesis. He was running out of research materials, too – a visit to the British Museum merely revealed that the unique collection of Revolutionary pamphlets deposited there by Croker was in a state of un-catalogued, unusable confusion. These difficulties would have been overcome. But the damp and chilly climate of Tocqueville's adored home was beginning to destroy him. In the summer of 1858 he began to spit blood and was ordered south by his doctors. He lingered too long in Normandy, unable to tear himself away; and after a disastrous journey, in atrocious winter conditions, arrived on the Riviera a dying man, though he had no suspicion of it. Duly, on 16 April 1859, at Cannes, he died.

De la Démocratie en Amérique, as we have seen, was published in two parts, the first in 1835, the second in 1840. The complete work is certainly a unity, but its development over a period of nine years (the preparatory work began when Tocqueville was on the way to America in 1831) and the profoundly different character of the two parts are sufficient reasons for considering them separately, without, however, losing sight of their essential oneness.

Démocratie I was written on the flood. Instinct had led Tocqueville to a task for which he was perfectly, one might say uniquely fitted. His prime object was to present the United States as the type of the coming order. As he remarked in his Introduction,

> In America I saw more than America; I looked for the image of democracy itself, its leanings, its character, its prejudices, its passions; I wanted to study it, if only to know what we have to hope for or to fear. (DA I 12)

He assumed before he sailed that the country he was to visit was in some sense a successful experiment; but not all the homework attempted in the hectic months before the voyage began could adequately prepare him for the reality. It burst on him like a new planet. It indeed proved that democracy was a feasible system of social and political organisation: this was to be the gospel that he brought triumphantly back. But America did more than that for him. Among other things he discovered that the transatlantic republicans had developed a flourishing school of political thought, fed by various streams from legal, historical and philosophical sources, which together formed a distinctive and advanced species of liberalism. *De la Démocratie en Amérique* was to be one of the channels by which this American tradition was fed into the European stream. Tocqueville also responded to the spectacle of the United States with creative joy. His notebooks are full of spontaneous portrayals of what it was like to be an American, to be in America – notes on the literature, religion, women, etc., which might, or might not, come in useful later on, but were for the moment recorded simply for their own enthralling sake. A child of the romantic age, he responded to the romance of America, to the Fenimore Cooper strain, and, while not suppressing the fact that the first Red Indian he saw was a drunk lying in the street at Buffalo, could still respond properly to the joys of a solitary journey with the Indian guide (and Beaumont, of course) through the untamed forest wilderness of Michigan. He also caught a more authentic note, the true romance of the frontier : he was never to forget winter in log-cabins on the Mississippi, and he liked the inhabitants, whose passion for dispensing information matched his own for acquiring it. He grew more and more excitedly convinced that America was a genuine laboratory of the future, and enthusiastically tested all his pet ideas there. When he set out to order his experiences into a book he decided that, in his own words, 'a new political science is necessary for an entirely new world.' (DA I 5) Drawing on Montesquieu, on Guizot, and on many other masters, he tried to supply that science. In his hands it turned out to be a brand of analytical sociology, though he did not call it that – Auguste Comte had only coined the word as recently as 1830, and it was not yet in general circulation.

Much of the foregoing is relevant to *Démocratie II*; but it is above all true of *Démocratie I*. The various impulses described were at their most intense immediately after Tocqueville's return from America in the spring of 1832, and did not flag while he drove himself to complete his book. The report on American prisons was left almost entirely to Beaumont; even French politics were scarcely allowed to distract. He continued to amass material, visiting England to find a specimen of a still-functioning aristocratic society to use as a control of the American democratic society, consulting American visitors to Paris, reading and re-reading important books and documents. His ambition was alight, he wrote in haste. It became clear that his chief problem was going to be the control of his material and ideas. So he disciplined himself severely, deciding to sacrifice everything to relevance and clarity. He relied on the boldness of his ideas, the freshness of his information, to give the book life – and his reliance was not unjustified. In places *Démocratie I* seems flat, both in matter and manner; but every such passage has its place in the grand design, and the reader is eventually forced to confess that he could not have done without them (for example, the lengthy description of the New England townships). Lucidity and intellectual coherence are among the strongest impressions left by the book.

Someone coming to it for the first time, however, will discover that it was beyond Tocqueville to subdue his inspiration into complete uniformity – nor can we be sorry that he failed. *De la Démocratie en Amérique* has all the depths, the layers, the contradictions of a work of genius, because it reflects the complexities of life. Much in its pages is wrong, much is irrelevant, all is rewarding. It is a book about democracy, and about America; it is a book about democracy in America; it is a book about America as democracy and democracy as America ... many of the decisions which shaped it were taken not by Tocqueville, or at least not by his conscious, painstaking, rational mind, but by his creative instinct. The book is therefore richer, but more difficult, than it would have been had his rational and sensible mode of writing been exactly adhered to. Sentences, paragraphs, pages, chapters and volumes follow logically on from each other; but all the time there is a deeper logic at work, and the results occasionally explode to the surface.

Démocratie I, as one might expect from the title, consists of a detailed and comprehensive survey of the political society of the United States. But it opens with an Introduction (written, like all introductions, after the work it introduces) which is perhaps the most important thing Tocqueville ever wrote. In it he tries not only to sum up what he has achieved and meant to achieve in his book but also to indicate his whole philosophy of history, politics and society. It is his *credo*, the place to which, above all others, enquirers may be sent to discover Tocqueville's strengths, his weaknesses, and, especially, his flavour, all epitomised in a little space. It is worth dwelling on here.

In his opening sentences he forcibly draws our attention to the most characteristic of his themes (and note how personally he does it, how the direct statement of Tocqueville the man and author, not sheltering behind the pompous masks of less sincere and talented authors, throws his point into sharp focus):

> Of all the novelties that attracted my attention during my stay in the United States, that which struck me most forcibly was the equality of condition among the people. I soon discovered that this basic fact had a prodigious influence on the development of society; it gave a special tone to the public mind, a special tenor to the laws; novel maxims to the governing authorities, particular customs to the governed. (DA I 1)

This equality of condition, he says, was so fundamental and important that its effects were felt in all departments of American life: it created opinions, gave birth to attitudes and feelings, suggested customs, and modified whatever it did not originate. But it was not merely the all-encompassing fact of American society. The development of equality of condition had been the chief factor in European and French society for the past seven hundred years. It was this perception, says Tocqueville, which gave birth to his book. He would set out to give an accurate picture of this great egalitarian revolution, and suggest the wisest ways of living with it. So much we gather from later pages; at the moment he is still chiefly concerned to establish his major hypothesis, the existence of a great egalitarian revolution whose roots lie far back in the past.

A great *egalitarian* revolution. Tocqueville calls it democratic. It had better be said at once that this confusion of terminology occurs again and again in his writing. The reader has constantly to ask himself what Tocqueville means, in any given instance, by his key terms. In *Démocratie II* the word *égalité* is used far more often than in *Démocratie I*: *démocratie* there means a system contrasted with aristocracy, *égalité* is its spirit. Even in *Démocratie II*, however, Tocqueville does not sufficiently distinguish between equality of conditions (a social fact or aspiration) and equality as an ethical idea. In *Démocratie I* he frequently uses the terms *démocratie*, *égalité* and *égalité des conditions* as if they were synonymous; as if, that is to say, he were only concerned with the principle of equality in its fullest sense: a sense comprising politics, social and economic status, intellectual and popular culture, etc. Yet he also employs *démo-*

cratie in the now traditional sense, to mean, in Lincoln's definition, government of the people, by the people, for the people.
Egalité is also often used as if it meant equality in political
rights only. A somewhat similar confusion hangs about Tocqueville's use of the word *république* and its derivatives. Part of the
time he uses it as synonymous with democratic government
(that is, popular self-government); part of the time as we use it
today, in opposition to the concept of monarchy ... It is hard
to excuse him for all these confusions. He might at least have
called his book *Equality in America* and so have given his
readers fair warning.

Instead he tries to prove the existence of his egalitarian
revolution by embarking on a grand survey of French history,
for that history, he asserts, is absolutely characteristic of the
history of the other Western nations. In a manner which shows
him to have been an historian born, he summarises the centuries in a few brilliant pages. To summarise them in turn is
beyond my ability. The general hypothesis is easy enough to
put over: Tocqueville does it himself when he says: 'If we
look over the pages of our national history, we shall find that
not a single great event of the past seven hundred years has
failed to promote equality of condition.' (DA I 3) To prove it,
he gives examples of how the Crusades, the Hundred Years
War, the rise of the Church, the monarchy, the cash nexus
and the middle class, among others, contributed to this effect.
Men, he concludes, have been blind instruments in the hand of
God:

> ... the gradual development of equality of condition is thus
> a work wrought by Providence, it has all the important
> characteristics: it is universal, it is lasting, it always eludes
> human control; all events and all men serve its furtherance.
> (DA I 4)

God is at work, says Tocqueville; if this is so it would be im-
pious to resist His decree; the Christian nations would be well-
advised to make the best of the egalitarian society that awaits
them.

What is one to make of this? It is probably best not to take
a high philosophical line over this passage. It will not do as a
serious argument about historical causation, but then Tocque-

ville probably did not mean it as such : at any rate, God's designs are rarely discussed in his later work. They are notoriously hard to fathom, and here it seems a fair comment that Tocqueville is trying to have it both ways – to reason from the rise of equality to the will of God, and from the will of God to the justification of the rise of equality. On the whole it seems likely that he was simply employing a rhetorical device that would appeal to his Christian, or at least deist readers and would thus enable him to convey his essential message : the urgency, the passion with which Tocqueville confronted the new era, and which he wanted his readers to share.

> You are reading a book the whole of which was written under the influence of a kind of religious terror produced in the soul of the author by the sight of this irresistible revolution, which has marched across so many centuries and so many obstacles, and which still today advances among the ruins it has made. (DA I 4)

This note of destiny is sounded repeatedly, not just in this Introduction, or in the rest of the *Démocratie*, but in everything he ever wrote. If equality seems to Tocqueville the key to the history of the West and to American society, his obsession with it must seem to us the key to Tocqueville. And it fits the lock. I have already sketched his historical predicament : he was an aristocrat whose time was up. In the *Démocratie*, and, at the end of his life, in the *Ancien Régime*, he is trying to persuade his countrymen, his fellow-nobles, his family, and, above all, himself, to see, to accept, and to co-operate with the coming democratic era.

But (we must ask) was he right? In what sense was the democratic order at hand? Fifteen years previously Hegel, in his *Philosophy of Right*, and later in his *Philosophy of History*, had come to rather different conclusions; it would not be very long before Marx produced a third hypothesis; Auguste Comte was at the very same time discerning the Technological Revolution. The idea of equality seemed obvious to Tocqueville; he was certain of the importance of the rise of the common man, the decline of the nobleman : he felt it in his blood. But posterity, with so many rival theories to choose from, and no aristocratic conditioning to affect its perceptions, must be less confident. Even if it is willing to preserve an open mind on the question, it will surely agree that the most important points about Tocqueville's grand scheme of history are that he believed it himself and that he found a large and appreciative audience for this belief among his contemporaries.

This fact, in turn, is easy to understand. However vague Tocqueville may have been, from time to time, in his usage, there can be no doubt that the sort of equality he was most interested in was, not equality of opportunity, equality before the law, or equality of property, but equality of status. He was concerned with influence, prestige, and power – especially political power. He wrote for a generation still wallowing in the wake of the great French Revolution, not to mention the wake of Napoleon and the 1830 Revolution. He was absolutely representative, not so much of the small band of liberal nobles as of the larger class to which they belonged, of intelligent, ambitious, public-spirited and prosperous Frenchmen who felt the will and the duty to govern, but knew all too clearly how much they had to lose – property, freedom, possibly their lives[1] – if they made mistakes. They were desperately in need of a guide. This Tocqueville set out to provide : 'A new political science is necessary for a new world.' (DA I 5) Such was his talent, such his good faith, that he persuaded them that he had actually provided it, and perhaps, for his generation, he had. They were still listening to him twenty years later. The remaining pages of his Introduction show why.

He sketches the possible democratic Utopia :

I imagine, then, a society in which all men, knowing the laws to be their own work, honour them and make no difficulty about submitting to them; in which the authority of government is respected as necessary and not as merely divine, in which the love felt for the head of the state is, not a passion, but a calm and reasoned sentiment. Each man having his rights, and being sure of keeping them, a manly confidence, a mutual respect, unites the classes, something as far removed from pride as from servility. Educated to perceive its true interests, the people understand that, in

[1]. Tocqueville's parents had narrowly escaped the guillotine during the Reign of Terror. Guizot's father had not been so lucky.

order to profit from the blessings of civil society, it is necessary to accept its burdens. The free association of citizens
replaces the individual power of nobles, and the state is
safe from both tyranny and licence ... if one finds less glory
than under an aristocracy, there is less wretchedness; pleas-
ures may be less intense, but well-being is more universal;
knowledge may be less profound, but ignorance is rarer;
passions less overwhelming, but behaviour more considerate;
more vice, less crime. (DA I 7)

France, he conceded, was far from this idyllic state; indeed, it
was just because this was so that he wrote with such urgency.
In cold and abstract language he drew a picture of French
society as it had emerged from the wreck of the old order. His
aristocratic prejudices, commonplace in the eighteenth century,
emerge in remarks like the following:

> I perceive that we have destroyed those individual powers
> which were able to struggle independently against tyranny;
> but I see that the government alone has inherited all the pre-
> rogatives torn from families, corporate institutions, and men:
> to the occasionally oppressive but frequently conservative
> power of a handful of citizens has thus succeeded the feeble-
> ness of all. (DA I 8)

The clash of rich and poor was bitter, and growing worse; the
poor were ignorant and selfish; the spell of royalty was broken,
the aristocracy had been destroyed, yet nothing replaced these
institutions; blind partisanship was wrecking the intellectual
world; religion was hopelessly compromised by reaction; the
virtuous and peaceable members of the nobility – society's
natural leaders – had succumbed to a purblind conservatism (a
hit at the Tocqueville family, this?); vulgar materialism was
rampant, and nothing seemed to be either forbidden or per-
mitted any longer, whether honourable or shameful, false or
true. In all this he was enunciating themes which were to
recur in his *Souvenirs* and his *Ancien Régime*.

However, there remained America, which showed not only
what was inevitable, but what was possible – showed that the
democratic Utopia was a real choice open to mankind, even to

French mankind. Let his readers, like himself, take courage from the transatlantic example.

With such a message, how could Tocqueville's grave sincerity fail to catch the public ear? Even today, when we know that his fears for the future were at least as well grounded as his hopes, it is still possible to feel that he has stated, as well as can be, the ideal of all men who believe, as he did, in the possibilities of man: who think that a free, ordered and egalitarian society is not necessarily a contradiction in terms. The fact that the path to a world order of peaceful democratic societies has proved even longer and thornier than he imagined does not oblige us to renounce the struggle forward. How much more , then, must his vision have attracted his own more hopeful, more anxious, less experienced generation.

Of course mere eloquence, however intelligent, would not have done the trick alone, or rather, would not have earned Tocqueville a great reputation. He anchored his hopes for the democratic future to the present success of democracy in America, and at the end of his Introduction invited his readers to go on and see how the American actuality validated European aspirations. Accordingly the rest of *Démocratie I* – the great bulk of the book – is formally an anatomy of the American republic. Here is a free people, says Tocqueville, enjoying in complete equality the complete range of political rights and social privileges; let us see how they organise themselves, how their liberty and equality affect their lives and manners, how successful or otherwise their experiment is, and what we can learn from it.

It is difficult, today, to do justice to the originality of Tocqueville's approach, which seemed so striking to his contemporaries. He had forerunners, of course, above all Montesquieu, perhaps as much the Montesquieu of the *Lettres Persanes* as the Montesquieu of the *Esprit des Lois*; but not even Montesquieu had been so systematic, so scholarly, and made such unquestionable additions to knowledge. America ceased to be a dream on the other side of the Atlantic: Tocqueville gave it weight, features, shape and size – made it a comprehensible polity. This was an immense service to his first readers; and though it would be risky to start a study of the United States with Tocqueville today, there is still much about that country which can best be learned from his pages.

Of course he is in many respects out of date, he made mistakes which every fool can now spot, and, above all, he has had innumerable imitators. Today we are most likely, I think, to be impressed by two things : first, by the extraordinary amount of knowledge that Tocqueville acquired and used; we sense, even if we have not read his papers, the vast number of books, articles and interviews that lies behind the simple statements of such chapters as that on the Federal Constitution; secondly, we must be struck by the way in which this scholarly and dispassionate survey is at the same time a continuation of the themes announced in the Introduction. By the end of *Démocratie I* we have learned as much about Tocqueville's world-picture as we have about the United States. So much is this the case that his America even assumes a slightly fictitious air, as if it were a creature of the imagination, like Plato's Republic. But of course this is a common feature of works of political thought.

His America is a country in which the people is sovereign; in which all institutions, and all customs, reflect, indeed proceed from, this fact, or so he asserts, explaining that

> the organisation of society is often determined by circumstances, sometimes by laws, most commonly by these two causes combined; but once it is in being it can itself be considered to be the prime cause of most of the laws, customs and ideas that control the behaviour of a nation; what it does not originate, it modifies. To understand the laws and manners of a people, then, we must begin by studying its social organisation. (DA I 45)

America is organised on the principle of popular sovereignty, and on the whole it works well, for, except in the south, the Americans have been, since their beginning, intelligent, educated, Protestant, self-respecting, self-reliant, middle-class, industrious and liberty-loving. Thanks to the absence of entail and primogeniture, which were abolished at the time of the American Revolution, the United States is a country like France, in which land holdings are generally uniform in size, thus giving a solid economic foundation to political equality (this is one of the points, by the way, where Tocqueville is largely mistaken and largely misleading). In short, the Americans have all the sustaining characteristics necessary to be successful democrats. Hence they were quite safe in adopting universal male suffrage.

Tocqueville next singles out the characteristic institutions of the American republic – the New England township, the basic unit (he thinks) of the whole; the country; the state; the federal Union. He shows how they all reflect certain assumptions : that the individual, to be free, must be independent, and is the best judge of his own interests; that for popular control to be effective, government must be decentralised, the minimum of power being conceded to the largest and remotest unit, the Union, the maximum to the smallest and nearest, the towns and counties; that officials need to be disciplined by frequent elections and by judicial supremacy; and that judges, to be responsive to the people in their own turn, must themselves be elected officials (though not, it is true, in the federal judicial system, where they are appointed to hold office during good behaviour). Tocqueville on the whole endorses all this, and is also most impressed by the grand jury, which he sees as the people in action. He likes bicameral legislatures too, such as he found in the United States, for by this means solid and experienced statesmen in one house can control the whims and passions of demagogues in the other. He goes so far as to call this sort of bicameralism 'an axiom of today's political science' (DA I 85), a statement hard to accept. He praises the whole system heartily, especially its principle of administrative decentralisation, so unlike the French way of doing things; and forcibly contrasts the public spirit, the schools, the churches and roads of American towns with the vegetable and slovenly condition of their French equivalents. But even if the concrete results did not favour the American system, he announces, he would still prefer it, since it is better to be free than efficient, however benevolent efficient autocrats may be. Local self-government gives men the habit of democracy, and resists the tendency, so evident in France since 1789, to place all power in the hands of the national government on the grounds that the government embodies the sovereign people. Democracy, he warns, is not necessarily decentralising : rather the reverse. Most earnestly he advises resistance to this trend.

On some points of the American system he is doubtful, but

on the whole reassuring. For example, he discusses the common European disapproval of elective executives (remembering the Polish monarchy) as opposed to hereditary ones. The elective Presidency, he explains, is no danger in a new country, inhabited by a people old in liberty, and anyway America has no strong external enemies and can afford a weak, subordinate and elective executive. He disapproves of the re-election of Presidents: the possibility of renewal dominates their minds too much, making them subservient to the whims of the majority; on the other hand, the separation of powers (executive, legislative, judicial) and the independence of the federal judges will protect the majority against its own mistakes. But Tocqueville is well aware – indeed it is his central theme, as we have seen – that these political mechanisms are dependent on a greater: on the people itself and its instituted sovereignty. In order to judge democracy in America, then, and to learn from it, it is necessary to analyse the Americans as well as American government: to supplement political science with sociology. And because Tocqueville is discussing the political character of the Americans, he starts with their partisan proclivities. These, he thinks, are much like those of the French: men are drawn either into the party of the democrats, or into that of the rich and aristocratic. Not that there is much of an aristocratic party in the United States nowadays (1835); it has been roundly beaten, and is driven to pretend conversion to democratic principles. The only overt parties left in the United States are not great ones based on the competing principles of aristocracy and democracy; they are mere base organisms competing for office. But the struggle between aristocracy and democracy continues, if in new forms.

The chapters that follow, dealing with the freedom of the press, political associations, and, vaguely, the government of democracy in America, scarcely seem at first to hang together or to follow on logically; but Tocqueville's purpose gradually becomes clear. He is trying to strike a balance: to see and state the good and the evil in American democracy, and to estimate, on this basis, its chances of survival. Rather than follow him through the windings and hesitations of his argument, it is better to sum him up boldly under these headings.

On the credit side Tocqueville puts many items. He admires

the freedom of the press, of course, suggesting that it positively strengthens the social fabric, and he is even more enthusiastic about the voluntary manner in which Americans associate together for good causes – this practice of association seems to him the essence of good citizenship. Democratic laws, he thinks, may be less well designed and executed than aristocratic ones, but (being designed solely to serve the interests of the majority) they are more just. The same is true of public officials, who may be less upright than aristocrats, but are checked by a more alert, well-informed and powerful public. Tocqueville denies that, as has been alleged, democracy favours all classes. No such government has yet been discovered. Society is divided into classes, and government must favour either the rich or the poor at the expense of the other.

> So what is the real advantage of democracy? It is not, as has been said, that it favours the prosperity of all, but only that it serves the well-being of the greatest number. (DA I 243)

(It is worth noting that here we have Tocqueville reasoning a bit like Marx and a bit like Bentham : all three were men of their age.) He goes on to remark that maladministration or corruption will be the work of elected individuals, and therefore temporary, in a democracy; in an aristocracy they will be the work of a class, labouring in its own interests, and therefore permanent. In a democracy, or at least in the American democracy, the instinctive patriotism which believes, feels, and acts has been replaced by a rational patriotism, grounded on self-interest : everyone has the vote, so everyone feels involved in, and responsible for, the actions of the state. This leads to a certain touchiness in the citizens, for they not only identify themselves with their country, work to improve it (from cupidity) and fight for it : each American, being in a sense responsible for his country, will praise and defend it against all comers. 'America is the land of freedom where, if he is to avoid giving offence, the foreigner cannot speak freely ...' (DA I 247) Tocqueville seems to think this a small matter. He also applauds the universal respect for law in America. Ceaseless political activity, involving every citizen, forces a man to think, to learn the limits of the possible, and, at the same time, by fortifying his self-respect, increases his sense of what he may achieve – no wonder the self-confident Americans are such good businessmen. The energetic pursuit of happiness is one of the greatest blessings brought by democracy. Democratic liberty encourages and stimulates men to achieve wonders, as a despotism cannot. A democratic government's projects may be more imperfect, but they will be more numerous, than those of a despotism. Finally, Tocqueville makes it clear that he prefers a system that increases the greater happiness of the greater number to any other, and identifies democracy as that system. His eloquence carries him to a dizzy pitch : it is no wonder that thereafter he consistently saw himself as the friend of democracy.

This did not stop him offering criticisms. And it must be conceded that if his defence of democracy is ultimately utilitarian, indeed Benthamite ('it is the greatest happiness of the greatest number that is the measure of right and wrong') then his criticisms are at bottom not merely aristocratic but élitist. It is therefore possible to argue that there was a fundamental contradiction in Tocqueville's attitudes; that he wanted to have it both ways, to have democracy with the characteristic virtues of aristocracy, or what he supposed to be such.

Democracy, he says, does not necessarily secure the services of the best men : the quality of American public men has declined with the rise of universal suffrage, for 'democratic' prejudices work against the election of persons of intellectual and moral superiority. There is no such thing as an official career, since you will lose your job if you lose an election : so good men do not offer to serve as professional administrators. Americans keep no archives or records except newspapers : their casualness makes the art of administration impossible. (This touching faith in the importance of paper reminds us that Tocqueville came from a bureaucratic family.) He sounds like Rousseau, who held that democracy was only fit for gods, when he says that 'democratic government, which is founded on such a simple and natural idea, presupposes, invariably, the existence of a very civilised and very well-informed society'. (DA I 215) Democratic government is more spendthrift than aristocracy, as it has more numerous and less prosperous supporters to satisfy. It will pay its senior officials less, its junior officials more. Americans, it is true, are parsimonious in public expenditure, but because of their commercial habits, not because of their democratic ones. The electorate cannot be bought, but politicians may be. Democracy is fine in times of peace, or when a sudden effort is necessary, but aristocracies are better at the long haul, since aristocrats feel present privations less sharply than poor democrats. It is, in fact, generally true that democrats find it difficult to defer present to secure future good. For similar reasons, aristocracies are better at the conduct of foreign policy, less likely to be carried away by ignorant passion.

There is some truth and some falsehood in these remarks: time has tested them thoroughly, and the reader can easily judge Tocqueville's accuracy and sagacity for himself. His most authentic doubts ran much deeper, and he turns to discuss them as soon as he has finished listing the real advantages of democracy. He derives them, like everything else, from what he elsewhere calls the sovereignty of the people, but now starts to name the omnipotence of the majority in the United States. He devotes a whole chapter to the consequences of the omnipotence of the majority, and describes them as baneful and dangerous. It is not only that frequent elections bring with them frequent alterations of state governments, laws and constitutions, making any steady course of government or administration impossible. There is also a real danger of tyranny – the tyranny of the majority.

This phrase is Tocqueville's single most famous contribution to political thought. It is an extremely strong one. To evaluate it justly the closest scrutiny is necessary. Above all, it is essential to understand what Tocqueville did *not* mean. He did *not* mean the tyranny of a large group over a smaller one – say, the tyranny so often exercised by American whites over American blacks. Nor would he have accepted that the oppression of English Catholics by English Protestants between the sixteenth and nineteenth centuries was a tyranny of the majority. It is even unlikely that he would have sided with those who claim that modern welfare states, in which the rich minority are taxed (some claim, over-taxed) for the benefit of the poor majority, are majority tyrannies. What worried Tocqueville was an imagined state in which a democratic majority, united in all points of belief, opinion, and conduct, might use its power

to oppress nonconformist minorities or nonconformist individuals. Tocqueville knew perfectly well that racial, religious or
economic conflicts can beget tyrannies, but that there was
nothing especially democratic about the fact. What worried
him was an evil that might arise solely in a democracy – in a
society where numbers were all. Was his anxiety well-founded?

In the first place we must note that Tocqueville, having
launched his striking phrase (which he seems to have evolved
from a passage in the *Federalist* papers by Hamilton and
Madison) produces singularly little empirical evidence to justify
it, though such a strong word as tyranny seems to need justification. However, in what he does say we can see the origins
of his concern.

> I know of no country where reign, generally speaking, less
> independence of mind, and less real freedom of discussion
> than America. There is no religious or political theory that
> cannot be freely urged in the constitutional states of Europe
> and that cannot penetrate into the others; for no country in
> Europe is so subdued to a single authority, that he who wants
> to tell the truth will not find there a support capable of
> maintaining him against the results of his unorthodoxy ... In
> America, the majority draws a mighty circle round all
> thought. Within its limits, the writer is free; but woe to him
> if he dares to cross them. (DA I 266)

The problem, we see, is scarcely political. What has struck
Tocqueville is the oppressive intellectual conformism of
American life (a problem still with us), and what we read is
his protest against it. So far, we may applaud his intelligence,
and insofar as his remarks also applied to the stifling society of
nineteenth-century France, we must concede a general applicability. But there remains the troublesome fact that he has been
guilty of gross over-statement.

For the word 'tyranny', if it is to mean anything at all, must
mean a personal or institutionalised system of *political* oppression. It should not be used, by a careful man (which we have
already seen that Tocqueville, where terminology is concerned,
was not) as synonymous with injustice or oppression. It is a
special form of these things. History provides an infinity of
examples. Not to look outside Tocqueville's own epoch, we can

see that both the Committee of Public Safety and Napoleon were tyrants: their power was not wholly illegitimate, but was substantially so, and was used largely for ends which no lover of justice or freedom can approve. Unfortunately these were both tyrannies of the minority, as most tyrannies have been. Tocqueville therefore took on a very paradoxical task in trying to show that there was, or could be, such a thing as tyranny of the majority. Apart from anything else, the exercise of tyranny, like the exercise of any form of political power, necessarily devolves on a minority of functionaries. Most citizens, most of the time, are too busy with getting a living even to wish to oppress each other. It is also a most notable fact of life in the liberal democracies with which Tocqueville was concerned, that while the majority will miraculously coalesce on polling day, it disperses the rest of the time, breaking up into a myriad of minorities; indeed, even on polling day the majority, which votes the winning party into office, though it calls itself Republican or Democratic, Conservative or Labour, is not the cohesive animal Tocqueville supposed, but a coalition of interest groups, painstakingly put together by party leaders, and held together with much difficulty. Its various shades find it hard to agree on anything except the desirability of winning an election. If this is tyranny, then the word is synonymous with freedom.

But it is scarcely necessary to belabour Tocqueville with facts, for he offered so few of his own. And this, like the success of his little phrase, is significant. John Stuart Mill took up the theme from Tocqueville, and it has been a delightful worry to conservatives ever since. The unreality of tyranny of the majority is matched by its psychological power. An unreal bogey, élitists like to frighten themselves with it, for reasons that will soon be clear.

'Omnipotence seems to me to be in itself a bad and dangerous thing,' says Tocqueville finely, in one of the key-sentences of the book. (DA I 263) He goes on to argue that in America the majority is legally irresistible (a more than doubtful proposition) and argues, in traditional fashion, for the desirability of the separation of powers as a check on it (but he does not notice that the US Constitution is also concerned to put checks on the power of minorities). A state in which the only checks on the majority are to be found, not in the laws, but in circumstances and manners is not good enough for him any more. He seems to have forgotten his original assertion of the priority of the social to the political: he has lost faith in his sociology. He is afraid that American officials, being entirely at the mercy of public opinion, and entrusted by the majority with sweeping powers, may one day become the instruments of majoritarian tyranny. The hard lot of writers has already been mentioned: they are turned into flatterers, statesmen into demagogues, by the omnipotence of the majority. Servility and adulation attend the sovereign American people as devoutly as they did Louis XIV. So the majority may one day over-reach itself, and drive minorities to desperate courses.

There is some sense, some accurate observation, even in this farrago of fright, which should be borne in mind when discussing its success. For it was very successful. It deeply impressed many of the *Démocratie*'s first readers. Most of them, cultivated ladies and gentlemen, living in a breathing-space between one revolution and another, were understandably alarmist; and Tocqueville was a skilful writer. It is depressing, all the same, to see how skin-deep was their liberalism. Conscious of belonging to the classes beleagured by the masses – even when, like Tocqueville, they were intellectually committed to democracy, both in the sense of government by the people and of social equality; even when they were convinced – perhaps because they were convinced – of its impending victory, they nonetheless dreaded it. Perhaps it was the expression of their guilt, or of their natural fear of change, or of their ignorance. Tocqueville, we have seen, wrote his book to reassure them. It is all the more saddening to find him, at this point, encouraging their timid delusions; and not at all surprising that they took his gloomy warnings to heart, even more than his encouragements.

So much for the readers. What of the writer? Certain things are immediately apparent. Tocqueville has trouble with the concept of 'the majority', failing, as usual, to face the problems of terminology. He never defines it, because its meaning seems too obvious. When he talks of tyranny of the majority it is clear, from the context, that he means by the majority, not the merely numerical majority he professes to be discussing, but the united majority of the ignorant, and, by the minority which they oppress, the minority of intelligent and enlightened persons symbolised by the writer. Americans, he says, are so fond of incense that they will persecute a writer who criticises them, by attacking his books, avoiding his company, and refusing to elect him to public office. Leaving aside all other questions for the moment, we must note that the majority's conduct, in this hypothetical case, hardly amounts to tyranny; and that it attacks the writer not because it is numerous, but because it is ignorant; not because it is strong, but because it is base. It is not clear that, in a democracy, these adjectives necessarily apply to the greater number of the people, not even clear that they applied to the majority of Americans in Tocqueville's day. The tendency of a numerical majority towards tyranny remains unproven. Nor does Tocqueville help himself by instancing a lynching, that occurred at Baltimore during the War of 1812. He does not show that it could not have happened under a monarchy or an aristocracy, or that it, or similar crimes, must have happened in non-American democracies. He gives an example of racial prejudice in Pennsylvania, to which the same objections apply; besides, who can seriously suppose that racial prejudice is a uniquely democratic vice? Tocqueville is so far from trying to argue this that the idea does not even cross his mind. He does, however, without realising it, drift into the error of assuming that because the majority of Americans are white, and oppress the minority who are not, this is an argument against majoritarian government. It is, of course, only an argument against Americans, and not all Americans at that. It was his favourite New England, which provided most of his cherished examples of democracy, that led the attack on slavery and racial oppression in the nineteenth century; the oligarchic South which led the defence.

But all this is somewhat beside the point, for Tocqueville gives the game away by harping so much on the oppression of writers. He is not really offering a reasoned critique of American democracy; he is expressing his fears that, under a democracy, he himself may not have a successful literary or political career in France. If he writes unpleasant truths about democracy, it is punishment by the French, not the American democrats that he fears: hence his frequent assertions that he writes as the friend, not the enemy, of democracy. His anxiety was encouraged, of course, by various Americans he met, still smarting at their defeat in elections by the friends of General Jackson; but even they, or some of them, when his book came out felt that he had gone much too far, for they really believed in the system of elections and majority rule. And it is amusing to note that when Tocqueville went into politics himself, he suppressed his haughty instincts as much as he could, and, as we have seen, not only proved himself a democrat, but was rewarded by being repeatedly re-elected.

Unhappily his book was not re-written, and from that day to this everyone with a grievance, real or fancied, against the American people, has found in Tocqueville a plausible, high-toned justification for complaining of tyranny. And the vanity of authors, who of course always deserve enormous sales, which only a conspiracy can cheat them out of, has been much soothed by his words. He himself was probably suffering from a professional hangover. An Enlightenment writer, born out of his due time, he was hankering for the irresponsibility of the eighteenth century. Then indeed authors who were not, like Rousseau, being hounded from country to country, or, like Diderot, engaged in a great capitalist enterprise such as the *Encyclopédie*, must have enjoyed a delicious sense of freedom, since whatever they wrote might be banned and would certainly have no immediate political effect. It must have come unpleasantly to such men to have to weigh their words and the effect of their words: to have to answer for their intelligence, information, good faith and sense of urgency before the bar of public opinion, not before a capricious and unintelligent censorship, or in the admiring hothouses of their pet *salons*.

Tocqueville then goes on to consider the restraints on the tyranny of the majority provided in the American system. Since the danger was imaginary we need not waste time on them; but it is worth remarking that so effective have these restraints proved that, from Tocqueville's day to our own, the tyrannies which most Americans have suffered from have been those of the minority, against which the Constitution offers at best inadequate shelter. (It has also proved poor protection against many abuses of power; but it takes more than a series of random tyrannous actions to establish the existence of a tyranny, which must be systematic.)

Finally Tocqueville settles down to consider the whole question of the future of the United States. His discussion is long and
subtle; here I need do no more than mention the stress he lays
of the manners (*mœurs*) and behaviour of the Americans –
the whole intellectual and moral life of a people. His stress on
this factor is one of his most important sociological insights.
He singles out American religion, culture, habits and practical
experience, discussing them with characteristic shrewdness.
After explaining, for example, the democratic tendencies of
American religion he adds that religion 'is sovereign over the
souls of women, and it is women who shape manners'.
(DA I 305) He concludes, in the end, as might be expected, that
American democracy is fairly sure of a long and successful
future, and gives his grounds for thinking that, with local
autonomy and strong religion, its success can be emulated in
Europe.

At this point he might have closed his book, since he had
clearly fulfilled his original plan. But throughout its course he
had been repeatedly tempted aside by topics not strictly necessary to his argument. For example, trained as a lawyer, he had
a professional fascination with the practice and principles of
American law, and while everything he has to say about the
judicial system is of the greatest interest, it is not always easy
to see what it has to do with his theme. Of this discursive
tendency Tocqueville became aware, and in the last chapter of
all set out boldly to consider topics which, being 'American
without being democratic', are connected with the main subject of his work (the laws and manners of American democracy)
but form no part of it. He takes up the race question, and
handles it brilliantly: what he writes is still one of the best
introductions to that tragic topic, all the better because he con-
siders the fate of the Indians as well as the Africans. Nowhere
is he more perceptive or more generous in his analysis. Next he
offers a discussion of the prospects of the Union, less impressive,
but interesting because, by its strong emphasis on states' rights
and state-patriotism, and its comparative scepticism about the
strength of national feeling ('The Union is an immense body
which offers only a vague object for patriotism to embrace'
DA I 383)) it shows how easy it was, early in the nineteenth
century, to miss the rising strength of American nationalism

which was so triumphantly to prove itself by winning the Civil War, the war for the Union. Tocqueville is bearish about the prospects of the Union, on various grounds, among them the coming conquest of the continent by American settlers (a process that, like democracy, he sees as proceeding from the hand of God), for he does not think the Union will be strong enough to control so vast an area. Democracy, on the other hand, being essential to the American people, where the Union is accidental, is certain of survival. And he hails the greatness of American democracy, not without a glance of pitying scorn at those in Europe who think they are democrats. Americans are great because, while accepting the rule of the majority, they acknowledge the superior power of the moral law, of humanity, justice and reason, and the legitimacy of vested rights. European democrats are to be despised because, among other villanies and follies, they suppose that tyranny is legitimate and in-justice holy, 'provided they are exercised in the name of the people'. (DA I 413) Perhaps he is thinking of the Jacobins, which prompts the guess that it was in France that he learned to fear the majority, America merely supplying, as he thought, addi-tional data. Such a process would explain his mistaking tyrannies of the minority for tyrannies of the majority. He has taken the Jacobins too much at their word, as if they were, not a tiny, tyrannous minority, but the huge majority that they claimed to be, or at least to accurately represent.

Even now Tocqueville has not quite done. With one of those prescient flashes for which he is famous, he predicts that the failure of democracy in America would be succeeded by per-sonal tyranny, not by a revival of aristocracy – the principle of aristocracy is dead. This was to come true in Tocqueville's lifetime, but in France, not in America. He discusses the causes of the commercial prosperity of the United States, in a chapter whose title gaily parodies Montesquieu; he makes some sharp remarks about Yankee merchants; sketches the reasons for the success of English, the failure of French colonisation in North America; and ends with his famous assertion that America, whose principle of action is liberty, and Russia, whose principle is servitude, will each one day hold in its hands the destinies of half the globe. We, today, may dismiss this as a lucky shot or praise it as showing an accurate sense of the drift of history:

the important thing to Tocqueville's contemporaries was its originality in suggesting that the struggling republic, built on dubious principles at the edge of the civilised world, would one day equal the great oriental military monarchy. Tocqueville could have found no more startling way of embodying his conviction that liberal democracy was on the march to power; and so with that thought he closed his book, and won the fame he longed for.

After such a mighty effort as that involved in producing a masterpiece, Tocqueville understandably took a rest, and was for some time hesitant about resuming work. He had originally meant to write a work in two parts, on democracy and politics, and on democracy and society, respectively. He turned away from this plan when Beaumont wrote his *Marie*, which Tocqueville saw as fulfilling the second part of his design. *Marie* was much less successful than *Démocratie I*, but what undermined Tocqueville's loyal restraint must rather have been the fact that *Marie*, whatever its virtues, was not a work by Alexis de Tocqueville. In short, he found himself still with a great deal of his own to say on democracy in America; and soon was back at his desk, saying it. The process of composition proved painful, and took much longer than his labours on the first volume had; but eventually the new book was finished, and published in 1840. It was received respectfully, but without the rapture that had greeted *Démocratie I*.

It is a very different thing. It was produced by toil, rather than by inspiration. The pressure of ideas and enthusiasm which so repeatedly distorted the shape, but enhanced the richness, of the first part, has slackened: Tocqueville keeps grimly and carefully to the main road. Nor does the second part have the sense of urgency of the first. No longer is the author trying to persuade his readers that democracy is a safe, just and inevitable political experiment, which must be successful, or tyranny will come. Now he is merely exploring the effects of equality of condition on feelings, opinions, and on the relations of men with each other in civil society: a comparatively academic exercise.

With Tocqueville, even academic exercises have great interest; but discussion of them is difficult. He had been an *a priori* writer even in *Démocratie I*; but there the tendency to extrapolate, to infer the actual from the hypothetical, was constantly checked and controlled by the weight of his empirical knowledge and his desires to impart it. This control has greatly weakened in *Démocratie II*. Tocqueville finds it necessary to open this new work with an assurance that he does *not* think that equality is 'the unique cause of everything that happens in our time': he is merely taking it as the theme of his book. But in practice the distinctive blurs and then vanishes. And it was far easier to infer what the consequences of egalitarianism *must be* than to ascertain what they actually were: his experimental laboratory, the United States, was not to be revisited. The reader of *Démocratie II* is thus constantly jolted. At times Tocqueville, reasoning from the speculative to the unknown, is boringly fanciful, and it becomes hard to forgive him for his solemnly pedagogical air. At other times some flash of insight, information or common sense will redeem him. The trouble is that it can never be predicted which way the worm will turn.

The difficulties may be illustrated by his remarks on religion, to be found in Book One, which is entitled *The influence of democracy on intellectual life in the United States*. This was a subject very close to Tocqueville's heart, as we know. Accordingly he was deeply interested by the manifestations of religion in the United States. Perhaps the oddest of all his experiences there was a meeting of the Shakers, a sect which jumped for Jesus, to the bafflement of Beaumont, Tocqueville, and a young Protestant American who was with them, and who remarked afterwards that two more spectacles of the same kind would make him turn Catholic. Unhappily this richly American scene, so redolent of its epoch, and indeed of revivalist American religion ever before and ever since, left no traces on the *Démocratie*. Tocqueville might have shed his Catholicism intellectually, but it was too much a part of his caste, country and childhood ever to be left behind in any other sense, and the questions he asks about religion in a democracy are those that any Catholic might put, though the answers are a little different. Dogmatic religious belief, Tocqueville holds, is necessary for human happiness; men, he thinks, have an immense interest in arriving at settled ideas of God, the soul, their duties to their Creator and their fellow-creatures, for 'doubt on these first principles would leave all their actions to chance and would condemn them to a great extent to anarchy and impotence'. (DA I 27) The trouble is that democracy fosters religious scepticism, and if it goes too far the people will, in the acuteness of their resultant spiritual misery, resolve to put an end to some of their troubles at least – the political ones – by submitting to a despot. So it is highly important that religion succeed in a democracy by confining itself to the moral and spiritual sphere; in an age of equality the idea of a single Creator is easily conceived, so it must not be confused by worship of the saints: it should have as simple an outward form as possible; it should modify, but not seek to destroy (since it can't, anyway) men's quest for material well-being; above all it must not cross swords with the ideas or interests of the majority except when absolutely necessary. If it acts like this, it will thrive, like the Catholic Church in the United States. Catholicism, indeed, has fine prospects in a democracy (thinks Tocqueville): equality makes men love to judge for themselves, but gives them also a taste for one unique social power, which is the same for all. This taste carries over into religion, and Catholicism is best suited to satisfy it. He concludes that the future will see democratic mankind divided into the sceptical and the Roman Catholic – unless, indeed, they succumb to the lures of pantheism, which Tocqueville sees as a terrible risk, a temptation peculiarly attractive to the democratic mind, one against which he calls all those who believe in the greatness of the human spirit to unite and fight.

What is one to say of this mixture of shrewdness and the higher silliness, except that it is typical of *Démocratie II*? An admirer of Tocqueville might point with justice to his reasoned case for the separation of church and state; certainly his account of the discretion with which the sects behave in America, and his analysis of the uniformity of religious belief, whatever the formal diversity of churches, is very much to the point, and rings true to all who know America. But his chapters on Catholicism and pantheism simply will not do; and his premiss that dogmatic religious belief is essential to human happiness is also unacceptable, for he seems to think that any belief is better than none, which can scarcely please those who stress the importance of right belief; and of course atheists and agnostics will laugh him out of court.

Another Tocquevillean preoccupation which comes to the

fore in *Démocratie II* in a way it did not in the first books is
the overt comparison of America with France. The restlessness
and egalitarianism of America have destroyed tradition, class,
and the influence of distinguished minds. Hence, says Tocqueville, Americans insist on judging everything for themselves —
though less so than the French, since American society is
stabilised by religion, and never experienced a democratic
revolution. Americans show greater aptitude and taste for
abstract ideas and Utopian theories than the English, because
the English are artistocratic; less than the French, because
while the Americans are a democratic people long experienced
in self-government (and there is nothing like the practice of
politics and government for blunting the appetite for abstrac-
tions) the French are a democratic people whose only contact
with any government, for an equally long time, has been purely
speculative There is not much harm in this sort of thing, and
not much good; but on Tocqueville it had the unfortunate
effect of insensibly leading him to confuse his categories. Long
ago Emile Faget commented on his tendency to attribute everything American to democracy; in *Démocratie II* he compounds
the mistake by calling France, too often, a democracy. He thus
slowly comes to assume that, where there is no obvious clash
between them, conditions in France and the United States are
the same, and universally true of democracies. As his *a priori*
method rises to loftier and loftier heights of abstract language
he conceals what he is doing better and better from himself;
and the resulting portrait bears very little resemblance to anything except the ensemble of Tocqueville's hopes and fears,
likes and dislikes.

Again, one begins to weary of the constant harping on the
contrast between aristocratic and democratic society. It is
almost as if Tocqueville had cast himself as an exile from an
imaginary world. At any rate the insolent regime of privilege
that France knew under the old order was dead long before he
wrote; his own allusions to the aristocratic or feudal system
show that he idealised it grossly, that in fact his reasonings
about aristocracy are as *a priori* as his reasonings about
democracy; but why does he have to go on at such length about
aristocracy at all? After all, his point of departure was his
belief that aristocracy, as a social system, was dead. Few of his

readers can have doubted this; why then did the author bore them by his constant reference to a dead part? As well try to write an illuminating book about constitutional monarchy to-day by constantly contrasting it with the divine monarchy of the sixteenth century. Thus Tocqueville launches a comparison of aristocratic with democratic literature. Aristocratic litera-ture, he finds, tends always to classicism and stagnation; demo-cratic literature to vigour and shallowness. Now, these observa-tions may be true, false, or meaningless (I think they are meaningless, but never mind). The point is, they are essentially trivial. Why did Tocqueville make them?

It would be easy to insinuate that he was overcome with nostalgia for a real or imagined aristocratic order; or that, back in the bosom of his thoroughly aristocratic friends and family, he succumbed to the delusion that there was still life in the ideals of the old order. There may be some truth in these sug-gestions. It seems to me more likely that Tocqueville was here falling into a trap of his own making. Committed as he was to the proposition that the effect of democracy (whether he meant liberalism or egalitarianism or both) was traceable in all areas of human life, he had constantly to fortify his sense of the phenomenon he was investigating by contrasting it with its antithesis, aristocracy. Otherwise, when discussing, say, litera-ture, he would insensibly have been drawn away from dis-cussing the characteristics of democratic literature to discussing the charactertistics of French or American or nineteenth-century literature. By forcing his perceptions into this strait-jacket he was true to his plan; the fact that he was false to truth, and that he thus ceased to be interesting, could distress him only if he noticed it.

Another handicap for a man discussing the influence of democracy on the intellect was his own limited intellectual range. Tocqueville had a severely specialised temperament, which led him, for edification, to works of history and politics, and for relaxation to works of French classical literature, or to such authors as Plutarch. He cared nothing for music in the age of Berlioz and Chopin, very little for painting, and not much more for modern fiction, poetry or drama. Consequently his comments on the arts, in *Démocratie II*, often seem a little beside the point. Thus he seeks to show that, under democracy, works of art multiply, but their merit diminishes; the noble is neglected in favour of the pretty. To illustrate these conten- tions he cites Raphael as an example of the sublime in art, David as an example of the sadly trivial. As to literature, he notices that America is dependent for its literature on Europe : 'There is scarcely one pioneer cabin where one cannot find an odd volume or two of Shakespeare. I remember having read, for the first time, the feudal drama of *Henry V* in a log-cabin.' (DA I 60) Tocqueville, it is true, does not attribute this fact wholly – only partially – to the sterility of democratic America, the fecundity of aristocratic Europe; but partially is bad enough; and he is so taken up with his obsessions that he fails to notice that *Henry V* is far more significant for its Anglo-Saxon nationalism than for its so-called feudal spirit. Later he sets out to show that the study of Greek and Latin literature is especially useful in democratic societies. It turns that he does not mean that the generality should study the ancient authors; no, ordinary people should concentrate on scientific, commer- cial and industrial subjects. Instead he thinks a study of ancient literature very necessary to correct the taste of modern, demo- cratic authors, whom he has earlier denounced as vulgarians. Unhappily he falls into inconsistency here : earlier we were told that the reason why modern, democratic writers were so slapdash, so unclassical, was that they necessarily had very little time to spare for literature. Where, then, are they sup- posed to find the leisure to take some polish from Theocritus and Virgil ?

It would be easy if tedious to elaborate these points, but surely unnecessary. It would be even easier to single out points where Tocqueville was right. The difficulty would remain, that both enterprises, Tocqueville's, and that of assessing him, are surely wastes of time. His method of proposing and establishing hypotheses is clearly, from a sociological point of view, wrong; and no one can really profit from sitting in a chair scoring for a clever marksman, who makes some hits but more misses (it being an off-day). The talents of reader and writer could be much better employed.

On the whole this verdict applies also to the remaining books of *Démocratie II*, in which Tocqueville discusses the influence of democracy on American attitudes; on American manners 'properly so-called'; and the influence of democratic thought and feeling on political society. It is scarcely necessary, then, to follow his course in any detail. It will be enough to pick out the half-dozen points on which he makes a real and original contribution to sociology and political science.

The first, and one of the most remarkable for the insight it displays, is Tocqueville's concept of *individualism*. This word, which seems so trite to us, was new in Tocqueville's day – invented, apparently, like so many other neologisms, by Comte. The meaning Tocqueville gave to it is very different from that we are are used to, but the process is familiar enough:

> Individualism is a considered, tranquil sentiment which leads each citizen to isolate himself from the mass of his fellows and retire, aloof, with his family and friends; in such a way that, after having thus created a little society for his own use, he willingly abandons the greater society to itself. (DA II 105)

It arises in a democratic society because such a society is far more mobile than traditional (Tocqueville, of course, says aristocratic), and though the duties of the citizen are plain, the duties of the private individual, as required by society, are much less so. Such an individual, quite probably uprooted from his native place and station, and with an independent economic position, loses his sense of belonging to the larger human family. Democracy thus 'throws each man on his sole resources, and threatens to shut him up in the solitude of his own heart'. (DA II 106)

The truth of this, in our day of anxieties induced by massive shifts of populations into new towns and new estates, the decay of the extended family, the loneliness of many old people and the restlessness of the young, does not need arguing: merely bearing in mind. Of equal interest is Tocqueville's favoured remedy, and still more the arguments by which he arrives at it. He begins his search for a cure by an assertion of his central political value, that of liberty. The manner in which he does so is highly significant, showing that for Tocqueville, at least, liberty is not merely negative freedom, but a state as positive as love or duty. Social equality, especially when promoted by the laws, reduces men to apathetic isolation from each other, to a state of individualism which can all too easily become outright selfishness. In such a condition they are not merely deluded (since in fact men do need each other for a hundred essential reasons) but apt material for a despot, who is only anxious that men should lose their sense of mutual interest and, sluggishly, leave everything to him. The despot wants quiet, docile, selfish subjects. The way to counter him, and to correct the evils he promotes, is to force men to be citizens. One such way is that of frequent elections. Tocqueville, clearly drawing on his American experience, gives an excellent account of the educative value of elections: they teach the rulers that they must depend on the ruled, and the ruled that they depend on each other, since, without votes, the one cannot get elected and the other cannot get the men they want into office. For such a great end the price of electoral politics – the intrigue, bitterness and ill-faith – is not too high. Again, swayed by American example, Tocqueville eagerly advocates local self-government. In the United States men have to govern themselves, in their townships, cities and states. Associated in this way for political purposes, they learn how to associate for other public, and private, ends. Freedom is thus with them an activity, not a mere condition; or, we might say, it is a value embodied in institutions. Its fruit is great public spirit and private benevolence. By dint of working for others, American citizens acquire the habit and the taste for it. Thus liberty, institutionalised, positive liberty, corrects the defects of equality, and indeed, in the last resort, is the best safeguard of equality itself, for, leaving other considerations out of it, in such a society as that described inequality, as well as despotism, would clearly find it hard to get a foothold.

Tocqueville also puts in a plea for enlightened self-interest as another corrective to individualism and selfishness. It is not, he thinks, wholly true, but almost wholly true, that what is right is also useful. Therefore it is worth educating the public in the belief that what it ought to do on general ethical grounds it ought also to do on prudential ones. Tocqueville does not want to run any risk of a society sliding into slavery from a failure to perceive its own interests.

For the rest, Tocqueville's achievement in the closing books of the *Démocratie* may be said to lie in three areas. In the first place he demonstrates his extreme intelligence and insight whenever he gives himself a chance by concentrating on a more or less factual issue. At one stage he remarks: 'Nothing so unproductive to the human mind as an abstract idea. I hasten to the facts, for an example will make my meaning clear . . .' He does not always obey his own precept, as we have seen; but where he does, the results remain impressive – as, for example, in his discussion of war, peace and armies in democratic societies, or in his simple but original remark that the reason why, in the American democracy, all jobs are considered equally honourable, is that all wages and salaries are paid in cash, not kind or service: so there is none of the anti-trade snobbery of Europe, where it is a hangover from the Middle Ages.

Secondly, Tocqueville's preoccupations, which he rides with a very loose rein, help us to build up a more detailed picture of his mind. Above all there is his concern with *égalité*, a concern at times so hostile as to give ammunition, and plenty of it, to anti-democrats, and so strong as eventually to attract the attention of the author himself, who, in the last book of *Démocratie II*, starts to backpedal with a vengeance, asserting that he sees the justice and therefore the beauty of equality, and even suggesting that it contains its built-in corrective to the tendencies to individualism, apathy and conformism earlier denounced: this corrective being precisely that restless search for independence and equality itself, which will not be content with anything less, this solvent of society, which Tocqueville has so repeatedly seemed to slight. Again, the same obsession, taking a different form, reinforces some of our earlier impressions by leading to repeated discussion of aristocratic society. By the end of the work we have been presented with an anatomy of aristocracy as well as of democracy. In part it is a refinement of Montesquieu, but, more interestingly, it is a clear idealisation of the pre-1789 world. We can see in the constant discussion of aristocratic manners, ideas and virtues how deep was Tocqueville's nostalgia for the secure world of his infancy; what we cannot see is a realistic picture of the European nobility of any time, any country. Following from this, naturally enough, is a deep dislike of revolutions: America is constantly congratulated on its good fortune in having reached democracy without revolution. But even here Tocqueville draws back at the brink: he finds it necessary to assert that resistance to government can be honest, and rebellion legitimate.

The reason for this is the most interesting of all. The great merit of *De la Démocratie en Amérique* is, after all, that it is anchored to the actual world of history: not for Tocqueville the affectation of timelessness that distinguishes such works as *The Republic* and *Leviathan*. He had written a tract for his times, and if, on occasion, his nostalgia and anxiety burst out and led him to write *against* his times, the whole disposition of his mind forced him to correct himself. He might fear that the new democratic world was not one in which a shy, scribbling aristocrat like himself could reasonably hope for political success; but his deep desire for such success, and the still deeper wish to perform some striking service for France, forbade him to succumb to his fears. Consequently he ends the book, not merely as he began, with a ringing affirmation of his faith as a liberal democrat, but with something very like a political programme – and one which was very practical in the sense that neither in principle nor, in many cases, in detail had the reforms he advocated been carried out or agreed to when he wrote.

This programme, if it deserves the name, can be found in *Démocratie II*, Book 2, chapter 7. Tocqueville begins by summing up the conclusions reached in earlier chapters about egalitarian society. It is easier to establish an absolute and despotic government in such a society than anywhere else. Such a government does not only oppress men, 'in the long run it will steal from each man several of the leading attributes of humanity.' (DA II 328) (In an earlier chapter Tocqueville talks of democratic despotism keeping men in a state of childishness.) Freedom and its qualities can counteract these tendencies. 'I would, I think, have loved liberty in all ages; but I feel inclined to adore it in the age in which we actually live.' (DA II 328) Since this is a democratic age, liberty cannot be based on aristocratic institutions any more (as, we may note, Montesquieu had argued in the *Esprit des Lois*): the sincere friend of freedom must equally be the sincere friend of equality if he is to succeed. 'So there is absolutely no question of reconstituting aristocratic society : the problem is to bring liberty to birth in the democratic society in which God has put us.' (DA II 328)

What, then, is to be done? Tocqueville has here brought himself to the brink of the pages to which the whole of *De la Démocratie en Amérique* is, in a sense, only a preparation. But so exhaustive has been his discussion that nothing of what he proposes can surprise an attentive reader. It is more important to note that the strength of his proposals can be assessed best by comparing them with the actual institutions of the July Monarchy, which in many crucial respects (for instance, freedom of the press) fell far behind what he thought desirable; the weakness, by comparison with the social and economic state of France under that monarchy, for Tocqueville has little or nothing to say that is pertinent to the problems of a working class struggling with the onset of the Industrial Revolution and the selfish, stupid oppression of the *haute bourgeoisie*. In short, had Tocqueville's advice been listened to, the Revolution of 1848 might have been averted; but the deepest problems of France would have remained.

Let us have democratically elected local authorities, he says, like the New England townships and town-meetings. Let us establish the right of free association, whether political, industrial, commercial, scientific or literary. Thus we will create powerful and enlightened groups which can act on government. (In other words, says the twentieth century, Tocqueville appreciates the democratic function of interest or pressure groups – but did he mean to endorse trades unions?) Freedom of the press is essential, for it provides the only sure means by which a victim of oppression can appeal to his nation or to the world for redress. A strong and independent judicial system, again as in America, is essential to protect the rights of the individual against a powerful, all-meddling state. Due process must be rigidly respected : it prevents the strong from immediately trampling the rights of the weak underfoot : between ruler and ruled, it gives the latter time to look about him. The rights of the individual are in fact the key to Tocqueville's system : he regards them as valuable in themselves, on the old, liberal grounds of natural law, and they must be encouraged precisely because it is the natural, revolutionary tendency of democracies to weaken respect for these rights in the name of social utility when they have outrun 'ordinary notions of equity and morality'. (DA II 333) Since revolutions invariably produce this phenomenon, they are to be discouraged, except in extreme cases of oppression.

Tocqueville concludes his great work by reaffirming his belief in democracy, his rejection of both defeatism and determinism. He concedes that the spectacle of a general mediocrity of humanity under democracy depresses him, but it does not therefore depress a better judge, God. 'It is natural to believe that what most satisfies the creator and preserver of men is not the prosperity of a few, but the greatest well-being of all : what seems to be decadence is therefore in His eyes progress; what pains me pleases Him. Equality is less sublime, perhaps, but it is more just, and its justice is its greatness and its beauty.' (DA II 337–8)

> I grow more and more attached to the belief that, to be honest and prosperous, democratic nations need only the will ... Providence has not created the human race entirely free, nor wholly slave. God sets, it is true, a fated circle round each man from which he cannot escape; but, within its vast limits, a man is powerful and free; and so are peoples.
>
> In our time the nations cannot choose social inequality; but it depends on them whether equality shall conduct them to servitude or to liberty, to civilisation or to barbarism, to prosperity or to wretchedness. (DA II 339)

And with that last challenge and warning he leaves, he says, the subject for ever.

Tocqueville may have thought he had done with democracy, but democracy had not done with him. He feared and detested revolutions, but was doomed to live through a big one. The calm hopes of the *Démocratie* were to be falsified, at least in the short run, and Tocqueville was not to live into the middle run, let alone the long. His advice to his countrymen under the July Monarchy was ignored, his political career was nipped in the bud by great and disasterous events. The rest of his intellectual life was to be taken up in grappling with these sad facts.

There can be no doubt that the Revolution of 1848 was a turning-point as much for Tocqueville as for France. For himself he could, he tells us, almost welcome it, for it put an end to the sterile parliamentary life of the July Monarchy in which he felt inadequate and helpless. But this was only a superficial response. He was too deeply committed to one view of history, indeed one view of France, not to regard its falsification by events as a personal, as well as a public disaster. It would be untrue to say that his books were thenceforth devoted merely to the explanation of catastrophe, the exploration of its roots. He remained Tocqueville, and the author of the *Ancien Régime* palpably shares many of the preoccupations of the author of the *Démocratie*. But to some extent the issues had changed, and new problems had come to the fore. The result was a different intellectual method – history rather than sociology; and a different hierarchy of urgency. Whereas before he had made it his business to enlarge principally on the dangers and opportunities of equality, now his chief preoccupation was the defence of liberty. Liberty had always been his goddess, of course; but not until 1848 did he feel that her inner shrine was endangered. On the contrary, says the *Souvenirs*, 'the general peacemaking and levelling that had followed that July Revolution had made me believe, for a long time, that I was destined to pass my life in an enervated and peaceful society.' (*Souv.* 35) As we have seen, he had supposed that France had completed

the revolutionary process, and become a truly democratic
society. After 1848, however, 'I began to think that in 1830 I
had taken the end of an act for the end of the play.' (*Souv*. 36)
The Revolution would continue, it seemed. Would it ever end?
He could not say, for

> I am weary of repeatedly mistaking cloudbanks for the shore,
> and now I often ask myself if the *terra firma* which we have
> sought so long really exists, and whether we are not doomed
> rather to struggle over the seas forever! (*Souv*. 87)

Sadly relinquishing all hope, for his lifetime, of the resumption
of peaceful progress towards a liberal democracy in France,
Tocqueville took up the task of vindicating the ideals by which
and for which he lived, and of discovering what were the real
difficulties in the way of realising them. For without such a
diagnosis of the disease there could be no cure.

He did not see his way ahead at once. The revolutionary
crisis which began in 1848 was not really resolved until the pro-
clamation of the Second Empire in 1852; the acute phase had
lasted until the *coup d'état* of 1851. So long as he was an active
politician, with a seat in the legislature, Tocqueville could not
commit himself wholly to writing again. But an imperative need
drove him to his desk, and, in the long periods of enforced
idleness imposed by his health during the dying days of the
Second Republic, he took up his pen once more, to write his
recollections.

The impulses which drive men to begin their memoirs are
legion. Tocqueville did his best to make his own motives clear:

> I am reduced, in this my solitude, to turning my thoughts
> on myself for a while, or rather to recalling the recent events
> in which I have played a part or which I have witnessed.
> The best employment of my leisure will be, it seems to me,
> to portray the men whose actions I have observed, to catch
> and to engrave on my memory, if I can, the confused traits
> which make up the blurred visage of my times. (*Souv*. 29)

He writes for his own enl'ghtenment, so the book must be
secret: he cannot afford to be less than frank, and he cannot be
frank if he has readers other than himself. And he will confine
himself to a limited period: to what happened between February

1848 and October 1849, since then only was he able to observe great events at close quarters.

So far so good; but Tocqueville begs more questions that he answers. Any reader of the *Souvenirs* soon discovers that Tocqueville wrote at least in part for the sheer joy of it; that he soon came to expect readers, if only posthumous ones (his will, we may note, contained instructions as to publication); above all, that he is not only concerned, as are all memoir writers, to explain and justify his conduct: he is primarily concerned to analyse and explain events themselves. The 1848 Revolution was a shattering affair: it presented an intellectual, moral and political challenge that Tocqueville could not ignore. He had predicted it; his prediction had been stunningly successful, having been vindicated within weeks, while men still remembered it. After the event, Tocqueville felt it incumbent on himself to show how and why he had made the prophecy and been correct, and why his interpretation was still valid. It is even possible to guess that, as the book progressed, his conception of it broadened and deepened: while sticking to his resolution not to write a chronicle of the revolution (an easy resolve to make, since neither his tastes nor his talents pointed that way) he did not feel debarred from attempting a history. He made notes of books and documents (principally the *Moniteur*, the official newspaper) to consult; he sought out former colleagues and noted down their versions of contentious events, or events that he himself had not witnessed. Underlying all, of course, was still the drive to explain, to himself and posterity, why liberty was worth cherishing, and how it had been threatened, indeed destroyed, in 1848: he had a passion to vindicate. But on this foundation of personal agony a large and noble edifice began to rise.

Unfortunately it was never completed. Tocqueville wrote the *Souvenirs* in three bursts, describing and analysing the fall of the July Monarchy, the first months of the Second Republic, and the history of the second Barrot ministry, in which he served (even this was not finished). He made notes for other topics he meant to cover; but that is all. Presumably he was too disheartened by the *coup d'état* to want to finish a work in which Louis Napoleon played so large a part. So we are left with nothing but an incomplete first draft. It says much about

Tocqueville that this first draft is nevertheless a masterpiece.

The *Souvenirs* should be read for the first time at one sitting, or at most two. It is the most immediately readable of Tocqueville's books; the most glittering; the most exciting, for it gallops the reader away on a headlong course through revolution and civil war. It is hard to say what at first sight one admires most – the cutting edge of the style, the memorable portraits of memorable men, the impetus of the narrative, or the serene intellectual grasp that relates the scurry of surface events to certain profound, and profoundly understood, forces in society. Tocqueville, by virtue of his peculiar intellectual gifts and tastes, achieves effortlessly what has defeated so many historians before and since, the convincing relationship of event to structure, of incident to trend, of the individual to the social, of the accidental to the inevitable. Perhaps one carries away, above all, an image of the author himself: for Tocqueville not only confines himself to matter of which he has first-hand knowledge, he repeatedly analyses his own motives and his place in the sweep of events.

At second or third glance the Souvenirs is less pleasing. Cool re-reading shows that, written, as it were, in the heat of battle, it is grossly partisan: in its pages all socialists are mad, all workers and revolutionaries are either deluded or villainous, and Tocqueville shoots them down with relish. The very brilliance of the portraits, with their combination of psychological insight and animal imagery – here a snake, there a vulture, elsewhere jackal-cum-ape – becomes repulsive, for it is too plain that Tocqueville exploits his insight to serve his malice. By no means the cruellest of such passages puts the Catholic statesman Montalembert in his place:

> The government had proposed to acquire all the railways by purchase. Montalembert opposed it: his case was good, but his speech was first-rate; I do not think I ever heard him speak better, before or since; of course I thought as he did, for once, but I am sure that even his adversaries would agree that he surpassed himself. He made a vigorous attack, but was less ill-tempered and insulting than usual. A touch of fear tempered his natural insolence and set limits on his perverse and combative vein, for, like many other men of

words, he had much greater boldness of language than stout-
ness of heart. (*Souv.* 153)

Here and elsewhere Tocqueville damns with faint praise and
loud damns. He gives unqualified praise only to his wife. Even
General Lamoricière, whom Tocqueville admires so much for
his good work in conquering Algeria and killing Parisians, has
faults which are carefully pointed out to us. Tocqueville is
severe on himself, it is true, but *qui s'accuse, s'excuse*; it
emerges all too plainly that he can forgive himself much more
easily than he can forgive others. Surely, the reader feels, the
political world of Paris cannot have been so exclusively inhabited by foolish knaves and knavish fools as Tocqueville
suggests? And, paradoxically, one of the finest passages of the
book, where Tocqueville suddenly asks himself whether the
future may not lie with socialism after all, for the sacred rights
of property are, when all is said and done, merely local and temporary arrangements, weakens the general effect, because elsewhere he knows no measure in his abuse of socialist designs
against property. At times he is snobbish. And in chapter XI,
book 2, which deals with his worst mistake – the part he
played in drafting the unworkable Constitution of the Second
Republic – he is positively evasive. Even his honesty, which
elsewhere is unquestionable, seems tainted.

Ultimately, of course, the verve and power of the *Souvenirs*
oblige us to forgive the author; but taking sides is anyway a
poor approach to a book. The wise historian will use this one
as an indispensable source for the history of nineteenth century
France; the student of Tocqueville as the key document in his
biography; the student of ideas for what it tells us of the changes
wrought by time and circumstances in the Tocquevillean
ideology. It is under the last heading that it must be considered
here.

From the first Tocqueville acknowledges that both the Revolution and his experience under Louis Philippe have forced him to
abandon one of the chief premisses of *De la Démocratie en
Amérique*. In his youth it had seemed that France was regaining
prosperity and greatness as it regained freedom, and he had
conceived the idea of 'a moderate, regulated liberty, controlled
by beliefs, manners and law; I felt the charm of this liberty:

it became the passion of my whole life'. (*Souv.* 86) 1830 had seemed to him, in his young hopefulness, to be the moment of final liberal triumph (Tocqueville seems to have forgotten how anxious about the future he had in fact been). The problem confronting the political societies of the West, he had stressed again and again, was that of coming to terms with the new democratic era. The basic Tocquevillean doctrine had been that democracy, to succeed in its own terms, must reconcile liberty and equality: if it did not it would succumb to tyranny, which was the enemy of both. However he did not think that it would succumb to tyranny, since the sweep of seven centuries was too strong to resist. 1830, he had thought at the time, was the culmination of this evolution, the opening of a new, duller, but juster and more peaceful era in human affairs.

This picture looked sadly battered after February 1848, which led Tocqueville to reassess the July Revolution and the ideas he had founded on it. Re-evaluating 1830 was the easy part. He now held that, by sweeping away the Bourbons, and their alliance of throne and altar – sword and chalice – *le rouge et le noir* – it had destroyed the last of the old order and given a complete triumph to the *bourgeoisie*. This triumph had been followed by a lull in events (which had misled Tocqueville) and a season of petty and selfish politics. But the reassessment of ideas was more far-reaching. It is, in fact, difficult to overstress the importance of the change in Tocqueville's views. It was profound. At one point, reflecting on the rôle of accident in history, he casts a shaft of dismissive irony at 'men of letters who have written history without having been involved in public business' and politicians 'who have always been concerned with generating events, never with describing them'. (*Souv.* 83) The former, says Tocqueville, see general causes in everything, the latter nothing but trivial ones. It is easy – perhaps too easy – to see a reflection here on the inexperienced author of *De la Démocratie en Amérique*, with his obsession about equality of condition. It is anyway striking that Tocqueville tacitly abandons, throughout the *Souvenirs*, his earlier formulation of the dynamic power of the march towards social equality. The word *égalité* scarcely occurs in this new book, and is certainly given no emphasis, either as an ideal or as a causative factor in events. It would be untrue to say that Tocqueville has discarded it entirely: but he has redefined it, radically altering its implications. His earlier theory implied greater concern about status than about material interests (possibly a clue to its great popularity in twentieth-century white middle-class America). Now he sees modern history as pushed by the competition of classes, a competition largely motored by desire for material possessions and well-being. At the risk of some slight distortion of his views (since he nowhere systematically expounds them) one might say that he has come to hold that originally there had been three classes: nobility, *bourgeoisie* and people. The continuous French Revolution destroyed the former ruling class, which was now no more than a freemasonry; it had no political significance any longer except when great events (for example, the June Days, 1848) roused it to memory of its former glory, and stirred it to perform a last service to France (in this example, taking the train from the countryside to Paris to fight rebellious workers). Its disappearance as an independent political factor, which had been the chief work of the Revolution in its first phase, the destruction of traditional privilege, had left the other two classes face to face.

Tocqueville is impartially severe on these other two classes. Never does he write more *en aristo* than when he describes the cupidity, the timidity, the personal and collective corruption of the French *bourgeoisie* that made it, under Louis Philippe, so deplorable a ruling class; unless when he describes the ignorance, rashness, frivolity, cruelty, and vulgar greed for possessions – the democratic disease of envy – which he attributes to the workers. He asserts, accurately enough, and repeatedly emphasizes, that the chief issue of politics is now the right of property; one side seeing it as the last surviving privilege, which must go like all the others; the other (with which Tocqueville aligns himself) seeing it as necessary to the stability of society, and ordained by the immutable laws of political economy. It might be argued that this is the same dispute over equality which had preoccupied the author of the *Démocratie*; but one significant difference makes the point worthless. Whereas in the *Démocratie* the materialism of democracy, the desire for possessions and well-being (*le bien-être*) is presented only as a part, and not an important or necessary part, of the search for equality, in the *Souvenirs* it has become the whole of it. This well evinces the radical change in the nature of Tocqueville's perceptions. He now resembles Marx, and has actually accepted the socialist propositions which underlie Marx's own speculations. The crucial difference is that Tocqueville does not believe that a redistribution of wealth and economic power along lines of greater equity is possible. He does not even think that the state can or should use its power to bring relief to the poor and unemployed, whether through the English device of a poor law or the French one of a national workshop. He is quite explicit in his repeated assertions that the workers who believe otherwise are ignorant fools who have been misled by ideological criminals: for example, at one point he says that 'Socialist theories continued to penetrate the popular mind in the form of greedy and envious passions.' (*Souv.* 178)

It is in passages like this that Tocqueville comes closest to being the conservative ideologist that American reactionaries are so anxious to prove him. Indeed, if that were all he had to say their case would be made, though their anxiety to make it would be baffling, since everything that has happened since 1848 has proved that the economic theories behind Tocqueville's thought on this point are as erroneous as the social opinions they support are heartless, indeed vicious (since no man has a right to believe and propagate theories which condemn fellow human beings to starvation and despair without end). Conservatives have nothing to gain by proving Tocqueville to have been as short-sighted, selfish and ignorant as themselves. And fortunately for him, he cannot be so easily reduced to fit their pint-pots.

For one thing, there is no necessary connection between his ideal of parliamentary liberty and his economic theory. In a Tocquevillean parliament liberty could be maintained and socialism be victorious, as indeed the coming of the welfare state has shown. It would be nice to think that Tocqueville would in the end have accepted the welfare state, had it come about in his lifetime. His objection to assaults on property was based squarely on his behalf that they were futile and socially disruptive. Had he been forced to abandon this belief, as his admirer John Stuart Mill was, he could scarcely, in logic, have stuck to his insistence on the absolute right of property. (But property tends to be a subject on which men's logic is shaky.)

Secondly, Tocqueville was too intelligent, in practice, to narrow his perceptions to the dimensions of his theory. As we have seen, he could even speculate that his theories of property rights would eventually become obsolete. And it will bear repeating that his central preoccupation was not property, but liberty – liberty and human dignity. It was these values that he saw as being increasingly endangered under the July Monarchy and the Second Republic, and to whose defence he rushed. Since men frequently write even better about what they love than about what they hate, it is the pages in the *Souvenirs* which testify to this love, and, still more, which analyse it, that remain most impressive.

It would have been open to Tocqueville to argue, as he felt the new revolution approach, that the time had come for the ruling clique of the July Monarchy to sink its differences and stand shoulder to shoulder – Guizot with Thiers, Barrot with Lamartine. Interestingly, he never did so, and only briefly, during the crisis leading up to the June Days, did he participate in such a movement of unity. The reason is plain : to someone of Tocqueville's beliefs, it was impossible to rally behind Guizot and Louis Philippe, since they would only exploit such a rallying to support their own policies, and it was those very policies which, by their blatant and cynical indecency, were hurrying on the crisis. Tocqueville, the student of the American democracy and the English aristocracy, was a profound believer in parliamentary institutions. They seemed to him to offer the best hope of peaceful progress : of a liberty regulated by law, of a government genuinely representative of the governed, which could respond to circumstances, to the wishes of its constituents, and make wise provision for the future. Parliamentary institutions, if honestly organised, also offered scope to talent and an honourable road to ambition. Under Guizot and Louis Philippe these criteria seemed to apply less and less. The electorate was tiny, and avowedly weighted in favour of the conservative, the rural and the rich. The government secured electoral victory by bribery and corruption, so that the country regarded parliamentary politics with contempt, and the parliamentarians themselves, feeling their impotence, were bored and restless (at this point of Tocqueville's analysis we catch an echo of Lamartine's famous assertion that 'La France est une nation qui s'ennuie'). The economic policies of the *régime* were retrograde, and its foreign policy one of humiliating, reactionary retreat – an especially dangerous matter, as Tocqueville emphasized, in a nation as proud and passionate as post-Napoleonic France. The way of salvation, the only way to avoid a revolution, was to adopt the principles and the programme of the liberal opposition : the programme, we might say, which Tocqueville himself had, as we have seen, advocated in the last pages of his *Démocratie*.

Why was it so important to avoid revolution? Again the answer is unequivocal. Tocqueville had a peculiarly lively sense of the connection between true liberty and true law. One might hazard a hundred reasons for this. Many of his relations had been butchered under a parody of due process during the Reign of Terror : his own parents had barely escaped death. He had seen, in America, a universal equation made between liberty and the law of the Constitution; had seen how Americans measured their freedom in terms of the laws which bound them; how all political questions in the end became legal ones, and were settled, amid general acquiescence, in the courts. He had been trained as a lawyer himself. He was a member of the possessing classes, and knew how much they stood to loose in a condition of social anarchy. Probably all and more than all these reasons conditioned his attitude. But the point to seize on is that he was right. The choice, he saw, was between unimpressive but real progress, under law, in which gains once made would not be forfeited; and a condition of naked class war, to be governed only by force, in which nothing was or could be secure for long – neither life, nor property, nor prosperity, nor above all, the passion of his life : liberty. In 1848 he foresaw, correctly, that 'whatever the lot of posterity, ours henceforward was to waste our life miserably amid alternate reactions of licence and oppression'. (*Souv.* 87) Renewed revolution in France would bring with it civil war and dictatorship. We must concede here that Tocqueville, in his dread of a left-wing dictatorship, not merely helped to bring about a right-wing dictatorship, but at first actively supported it, when it was wielded by his hero, General Cavaignac, or by the Barrot Cabinet of which he was a member, in conjunction with Louis Napoleon. Nor, as we have seen, did he refrain from taking sides fiercely in the civil war, much though he deplored its coming. But he expiated any charge of inconsistency, though not of inhumanity, by the earnestness and determination with which he opposed Louis Napoleon's dictatorship after 1849. There can be no doubt that he was conscientiously opposed to *any* government which rested on force and fraud, rather than on law and consent.

His comments, then, on the men who brought about the February Revolution, are justly bitter. A stupidly oppressive government; a stupidly rash opposition (he is very severe on the Banquets agitation); together brought about disaster, and together receive his angry condemnation. He records, with sombre satisfaction, at the end of his account of the fall of the July Monarchy, that

> Of the four men who contributed most to bring about the events of the 24th of February, Louis-Philippe, M. Guizot, M. Thiers and M. Barrot, the two first were proscribed at the end of the same day, and the two others were half-mad. (*Souv.* 80)

Justice was done, though the heavens had fallen. At the same time, he lists and stresses the general causes which underlay the occasions of the Revolution. This list is especially interesting, for it shows Tocqueville shifting from the speculative, almost intuitive sociology of *De la Démocratie en Amérique* to the historical approach of the *Ancien Régime*. Thus, some of his general causes are old familiars: centralisation, and the instability which has known seven revolutions in less than sixty years (we remember America's good fortune in enjoying vigorous local self-government and in being a democracy without having endured a democratic revolution). He mentions the Industrial Revolution for the first time; it generated, he says, a large pool of unemployment in Paris (he does not discuss the depression of 1846–7). He insists, of course, on the false socialist theories which misled a multitude taught to be greedy by the July Monarchy and 'the democratic disease of envy'. He points to the contempt in which the ruling class was held, especially its leaders, a contempt so universal that, as he brilliantly perceives, 'it paralysed the resistance even of these who had the

greatest interest in maintaining the power which it was sub-
verting'. (*Souv*. 84)

Tocqueville, then, greeted the February Revolution with deep
dismay, and his opinion of his countrymen, for their weakness in letting it come about, plummeted. They had thrown
away law and liberty; and thus had shown themselves un-
worthy of liberty – impatient, rash, contemptuous of law,
frivolous in everything. On the other hand, he adapted to the
coming of the Second Republic with surprising ease. He
remained theoretically a supporter of constitutional monarchy
as the best guarantee of stability and law, but in practice he
became, and remained, a firm republican. The Republic was
better than any of the possible alternatives: above all, it was
better than socialism or Bonapartism. Accordingly, the second
half of the *Souvenirs* is primarily concerned with depicting
Tocqueville's efforts to carve a career for himself in the new
order. To a biographer or other student of Tocqueville's life
and character these passages are endlessly fascinating, for they
display with crystal clarity Tocqueville's strength and weakness as a politician. To the student of his ideas, however, they
have less to offer. The acuteness of his intelligence means that
he continues to throw off striking observations about the practice of liberal politics in republican France, and about the
course of the February Revolution: observations which still
have point. For example, M. Raymond Aron has pounced on
Tocqueville's repeated observation that the participants in
1848 were all too often merely aping their predecessors,
whether Jacobin or Girondin: M. Aron alleges that a similar
psychodrama (his term) was played out in Paris in 1968, and
demonstrates the futility of the young would-be revolutionaries
of that year, as Tocqueville demonstrated the futility of his own
contemporaries. But on the whole only one theme remains to
be noted, one that provides the bridge to the *Ancien Régime*:
centralisation.

This was an idea by no means absent from the *Démocratie*.
But in the *Souvenirs* it acquires a new importance, which it is
to retain until the end of Tocqueville's working life. It has
become the principal source of evil, the chief danger to liberty.
It is time to examine the reasons given for this at first sight
implausible and startling contention.

The *Démocratie* had been concerned, not with America as such, let alone France as such, but with the idea of an egalitarian, democratic state such as had nowhere yet come wholly into existence. To that extent it was, as we have seen, a synthetic, Utopian, anti-empirical book, and it is not surprising that the applicability of its doctrines, and the balance struck between them, were discovered to vary in the context of actual societies. It would be easy to argue that Tocqueville's resort to historical analysis, in both the *Souvenirs* and the *Ancien Régime*, was a deliberate criticism of the more abstract method of the *Démocratie*: unhappily it would also be dishonest, for Tocqueville never disavowed the approach and techniques of his masterpiece (though he did talk of it as his book on America, thereby acknowledging what its most valuable portions were). But undoubtedly he did in practice discover, as we have seen, that the problems caused by the coming of political and social equality could be left aside in France for the time, since equality had not, after all, arrived, even under the Republic, 'democratic, one, and indivisible' as it called itself; while liberty was far from safe. Casting about for an explanation, Tocqueville settled on administrative centralisation.

There were certain obvious predispositions favouring such a view. One of the chief themes of the *Souvenirs* is that France was saved from the socialists of Paris by the splendid efforts of the provinces. Indeed, so devoted is Tocqueville to the good work done in the June Days by men like his own aristocratic, clerical or peasant – in any case deeply conservative – constituents that we discover that he does not altogether accept the division of France into two classes, *bourgeoisie* and wage-earners, that he seems to believe in elsewhere. There is at least one other class – the peasantry; and had Tocqueville followed the logic of his own views a little more thoroughly he could hardly have failed, one would suppose, to come upon some theory of urbanisation as a major factor in French history: for it was not only in Paris that a class-war was developing – Lyons, for one, furnished other bloody illustrations of the state. But Tocqueville never mentions Lyons, and greatly underplays the revolutionary movement in the provinces. It is true that he took over the concept of the industrial revolution from the socialists in his analysis of the causes of the February Revolution. But of course urbanism and industrialisation are not necessarily connected with centralisation, as the history of England, America and Germany illustrates. To that extent, then, Tocqueville's attachment to the centralisation hypothesis must be seen as evidence that he had not accurately seen and stated the problem.

It must be remembered, however, that he was less concerned to account for the 1848 Revolution than for the social and political predicament in which France laboured long before and long after that event. To his mind, administrative centralisation was certainly one of the evil aspects of the July Monarchy against which France rebelled; but it effortlessly survived Louis Philippe, as it had so many earlier rulers. And while it endured, liberty was unsafe.

In the *Démocratie* he had carefully distinguished between two sorts of centralisation : *governmental*, necessary to carry out a nation's foreign policy, and to execute its general laws, and *administrative*, by which local government is also carried on from the national centre. This distinction looks neater than it is, since it is often difficult to tell where one realm of action begins and another ends, and Tocqueville very often seems to be against all centralisation whatever (though he would certainly have repudiated this charge with vehemence). In short, here as elsewhere, Tocqueville's terminology lets him down. But his drift is clear. His dislike of administrative centralisation, both in the *Démocratie* and the *Souvenirs*, is the other side of the coin of his enthusiasm for self-government and independence, whether national, local or personal – his own sort of positive liberty. He wholeheartedly supported Lamennais' doctrine, enunciated during the first meeting of the constitutional committee of 1848, that 'a republic, the citizens of which lacked the intelligence and the daily practice to look after themselves, was a monster which could not live', as well he might, since it summed up the message of the *Démocratie*. Tocqueville, with his memories of the vigorous townships of New England, never lost his feeling that this was the true republican liberty, nor his wish to plant it in France. And he reasoned that the long French history of decision-making from the centre, a practice which had grown stronger, if anything, in recent times, was a major obstacle in the way of this sturdy self-reliance, as well as being a powerful instrument of oppression. He does not seem to have foreseen the purely technical necessities which in modern times have so greatly fostered the powers of central governments in all countries, democratic or not; but it is doubtful if he would have accepted them as a sufficient justification of a deplorable development. At least Tocqueville would have fought a sturdy rearguard action, as anyone who professes to share his vision ought to do. For he was always far more concerned with the moral status of a political system than anything else. 'Liberty and human dignity' necessitated, in his eyes, self-respect and self-government, and neither are conspicuously well-served by the bureaucracies of Leviathan. As to France in particular, events have given too much support to his gloomy observation that 'in France, there is just about one thing only that we cannot build : a free government, and only one institution that we cannot destroy : centralisation'. (*Souv.* 182)

But none of this explains the passion with which centralisation is singled out for condemnation in the *Souvenirs*. It is, in fact, idle to look for deep philosophical reasons. Tocqueville was by now more concerned with historical actualities. However it had sprung up, French administrative centralisation was a fact, and had proved, from the time of Napoleon onwards, an apt instrument for tyranny, folly and faction. Who ruled Paris ruled France; and it seemed to Tocqueville that, given such a state of affairs, and the sort of accidents which repeatedly occurred to topple governments in Paris, one need look no further for the worst enemy of liberty. About the only encouraging episode in the 1848 revolution, from this point of view as from any other, was the successful mutiny of the provinces against Paris in the June Days (it is appalling to think what he would have made of the Commune). If it did nothing else, this mutiny gave a breathing-space in which the Republic and democracy could attempt to establish themselves. But, he argued, their victory could only be shallow and temporary (as indeed it proved) unless it was associated with a growth in republican manners, government and opinions at all levels and in all areas. For this reason his failure to secure any decentralising or devolutionary provisions in the new constitution was a major defeat for his beliefs; and so it did not surprise him that, in 1851, it was again proved that the master of Paris was the dictator of France : Louis

Napoleon's *coup*, having succeeded at the centre, could not be resisted on the periphery. Q.E.D.

Still, the question remained; as a practical matter, how could, or should, or might France be induced to abandon centralisation? To Tocqueville this implied a preliminary question: how had the monster come into being? This was essentially a historical enquiry; so his next blow in the long battle for liberty was a historical study devoted to just this topic.

To his faithful reader, Tocqueville's *Ancien Régime* is full of familiarities as well as surprises. It is full of themes introduced in earlier work and in some independence of each other, which are now presented together. The last book which Tocqueville lived to complete, it is the crown of a career and a farewell. It is as a farewell that it will be discussed here.

Other approaches would be possible. For instance, the *Ancien Régime* is avowedly a work of history. As such it must submit to the usual tests, of accuracy, insight, and fullness of information. It does not, truth to tell, survive these tests, as we apply them in the late twentieth century, with flags flying. There was much about his chosen theme that Tocqueville could not, or at any rate did not, know. Some things he seems to have forgotten, so that he made mistakes which are superficially unaccountable. Thus, is spite of some brilliant pages on international relations, and the rôle of armies in politics, in the third part of the *Souvenirs*, he nowhere even hints, in the *Ancien Régime*, that the necessity of an armed force to defend the frontiers had anything to do with the growth of centralisation and monarchical power in France. In fact we can argue that he did not write so good a historical work as he might : but then who does? It would reflect oddly on the diligence of more than a century if today's historians could not correct Tocqueville on innumerable points, even to the extent of pointing out where, on the basis of information available to him, he went wrong – let alone where he went wrong from not knowing what remained undiscovered for another fifty or a hundred years. It is high praise of the *Ancien Régime* to say that it still makes a good introduction to the advanced study of its subject; it would be folly to claim more. No one today should set out to learn about eighteenth-century France from a nineteenth-century writer.

As we have seen, the *Ancien Régime* arose out of Tocqueville's concern with his own times, not with the past as such. It was partly an attack on Bonapartism. The modern historian is therefore entitled to approach it as a document for the study of the nineteenth century. He may scrutinise it to discover what he can about France and French political thought under the Second Empire; he may, indeed he should, interpret it in the light of what we know about Napoleon III. Again, if he does so, Tocqueville will not emerge unscathed: we can see virtues in that ruler, and vices in the position of his critics, to which Tocqueville was blind. This approach, and still more a purely biographical one, relating the structure and details of the book to the course of Tocqueville's life and studies in the last decade of his life, get far closer to the author's essence than the merely historiographical one. It would also be possible to approach the book as a literary critic, and show how, like many other obsolete works of history which are not in themselves primary sources (say, Macaulay or Gibbon) it can still afford keen and high enjoyment to the intelligent reader. But all such methods will be eschewed here. It is my contention that the *Ancien Régime* is in the first place the summation of a life's beliefs; it is best understood in the context provided by the ideas of the *Démocratie* and the *Souvenirs*. As much as its predecessors it is a volume of doctrine; it is a last sermon. What does it say?

Much what was said before, of course. It opens, as the *Démocratie* had done, with an overture – a Foreword in which Tocqueville states, with absolute clarity, what he is about. In the first place he denies that he is writing a history of the Revolution, by which he seems to understand a political chronicle: he is writing 'une étude sur cette Révolution'. His qualms about claiming the name of historian are interesting, for they show how conscious he was of his originality in seeking to write what we would now call social history, and of his preaching mission. Perhaps he wondered, for a moment, if it was really the historian's business to use the past as a rod on the back of the present; but, if so, he was not deterred for long: he whacks away with a will. He has been studying, he tells us, the means by which the French, while deluding themselves that they had overthrown the old order for ever, in fact reconstituted it on a new basis. There was for more continuity between eighteenth- and nineteenth-century France than was commonly supposed. The work of the Revolution had been chiefly to destroy aristocracy and thus to create an egalitarian society the members of which, isolated individuals, were defenceless against despotism and abandoned to the lust for gain. For such a state of affairs the only corrective is liberty. It alone can draw citizens

> out of the isolation in which the very independence of their condition forced them to live, and constrain them to work together, revive the warmth of their feelings for each other, and daily bring them together by the necessity of understanding each other, of persuading each other and of satisfying each other in matters of common concern. (AR 75)

Liberty alone can lift men's souls above the petty pursuit of gain to contemplate larger and nobler ends. Prosperity and private virtue can flourish under democratic despotism,

> but I would go so far as to say that one will never see, in such societies, great citizens or a great people, indeed I fear that hearts and minds grow continually more degraded where equality and despotism are joined. (AR 75)

This is unfashionable doctrine, Tocqueville alleges, but surely it has universal appeal. Surely everyone must prefer self-government to slavery? 'Even despots do not deny the excellence of liberty; only they wish to keep it to themselves.' (AR 75–6) Only a contempt for the human race, a view that it is unfit for liberty, could make despotism seem desirable; and 'I ask to be allowed to wait a little longer before adopting that attitude'. (AR 76)

Two aspects of this Foreword leap to the eye. In the first place, little of it is new. An exception, an important one, is Tocqueville's newly expressed belief that an aristocracy, wielding power independent of the government, is a valuable check on despotism. Even this was mentioned in the *Démocratie*, and it was an eighteenth-century commonplace which Tocqueville could have found in, for example, his much-admired Montesquieu, who praised aristocracies as intermediate bodies protecting kings against people, people against kings. What is new is the very strong language in which Tocqueville presses this doctrine: 'among the world's societies, those which will always have the greatest difficulty in escaping from absolutism for long are precisely those societies in which aristocracy can exist no longer'. (AR 74) The implications of this belief are discussed below. For the moment, we need do no more than note that the defenceless and selfish individualism which Tocqueville here deplores was first attacked in the *Démocratie*; that lust for material gain was the chief object of his attack under the July Monarchy; that the equation of egalitarianism with materialism was first made in the *Souvenirs*; that the celebration of liberty and the denunciation of despotism represent the two sides of Tocqueville's deepest conviction; that, in short, he is quite right to claim that he has scarcely changed his position after twenty years. Such modifications as have been made are slight. Whereas the *Démocratie* was an encouraging demonstration of how the Americans gained and kept their liberty, so the *Ancien Régime* is planned to be a gloomy exposition of how the French lost theirs, and lost even the appetite for it. Tocqueville is as polemical in the cause of liberty as ever.

Secondly, the Foreword proves that he is as deeply concerned with the nineteenth century as with the eighteenth. Tocqueville wrote steadily with his eye on the, to him, deplorable condition of France under Napoleon III. The attack on despotism could be misunderstood by none of his original readers; his sketch of the main development of French history since 1789, which shows a people abandoning their generous dreams of liberty for the poisoned benefits of life under the tyranny of Napoleon I, made the same point. To avoid all possible mistake, Tocqueville carefully stated: 'I confess that in studying the anatomy of our old social system I have never entirely lost sight of the new. I have wanted not only to see what the invalid died of, but how he might have been saved from death.' (AR 73) If he lives to complete the work projected – his great study of the Revolution from beginning to end – he will also examine the new state of society, 'will try and decide in what ways it is like its predecessor, in what it differs, what we lost in that immense convulsion, what we gained, and, finally, I will try to catch a glimpse of our future'. (AR 72–3)

After this we cannot say that we have not been warned. Tocqueville is avowedly setting out to write tendentious history, and not all his emphasis on his work in central and provincial archives, nor our trust in his intellectual integrity should allow

us to forget this fact for a moment. If, in the past, it has nevertheless been frequently overlooked, it is because the *Ancien
Régime* is only a fragment of the much larger work planned.

Apart from the Foreword, Book One is the only finished por-
tion linking the *Ancien Régime* as we have it to the grand
design. It is concerned to establish Tocqueville's definition of
the Revolution as a European phenomenon, and to lay down its
general causes. Tocqueville paints with a broad brush. The
Revolution, he says, seemed at first a trivial and then, soon
after, a terrible event: what Burke called 'this strange and
hideous phantom'. It seemed an assault on all religion, on all
civil and political order:

> it was possible to believe that its result would be the destruc-
> tion, not merely of a particular system of social organisation,
> but of all order; not just of a government, but of all social
> authorities; it was possible to think that its nature was
> essentially anarchic. (AR 85)

This, says Tocqueville, was to mistake its nature. The object of
its attack was the so-called old order (*ancien régime*) – the
aristocratic organisation of European society that had prevailed
for a millenium, and was now to succumb to the onslaught of
the egalitarian passion. (Here we note the re-emergence of a
Tocqueville *leitmotiv*.) Once satisfied, this egalitarian passion
had nothing against either religion or strong government, as
subsequent events had shown. Christianity throve under democracy (here is the old confusion of terms) and so did strong
central government – even autocratic monarchs had come to
perceive the immense power that the abolition of privilege
added to their thrones (Tocqueville had been much impressed,
during the Revolution of 1848, by the way in which feudal
rights in central Europe, abolished by the rising of the peasantry, were not restored when the monarchs regained control). It
had been the universal appeal of the egalitarian cause that had
enabled the French Revolution to make light of frontiers, laws,
languages and traditions. In this it was more like a religious
revolution than a political one, for, like a religion (say, Islam or
Christianity) it concerned itself with human nature pure and
simple, being based on general principles; on the rights, not of
Frenchmen only, but of Man. The Revolution,

by basing itself always on the most universal, least particular, principles, and on what we may call the most 'natural' forms of state and government, made itself comprehensible to all men everywhere and imitable in a hundred places at the same time. (AR 89)

But it would have got nowhere if many nations had not simultaneously reached a stage in their development when the appeal of the Revolution could be understood, felt, and responded to. Almost all European nations from the Polish frontier to the Irish Sea had had the same institutions, which were now breaking down. In spite of local variations, the old order was the same everywhere, and declined equally everywhere. In France, England and Germany this 'ancient constitution of Europe' (AR 92) was breaking down by mid-eighteenth century. The Revolution came to destroy it forever.

What, then, was the Revolution? Tocqueville's answer was clear, and the reader who has been following the development of his thought will have no difficulty in foreseeing it. The Revolution, he says, was essentially social and political: its tendency was to increase the power and rights of public authority, in the sacred name of equality. The destruction of the old aristocratic order seemed more radical than it was, since so much else got involved in it; but that order would have collapsed anyway. The Revolution in France and Europe was simply the violent expression and sudden achievement of changes that had been maturing for six generations.

A rapid summary cannot really do justice to the brilliance and profundity of these pages of Tocqueville; but it is perhaps enough to add that his picture is still acceptable – indeed, in my opinion, is still the only substantially valid interpretation of the great convulsion we call the Revolution. The old order *was* 'feudal', 'aristocratic', or what you will; it *was* replaced, in all those countries where it made itself effective, by strong centralised nation-states, basing themselves on the principle of equality before the law – or, as Tocqueville would add at this point, equality under the despot.

It will be seen that, at least in its language, this picture does not differ substantially from that sketched in the Introduction to the *Démocratie* : equality of condition is the motor of history still. What is not clear in these pages is whether Tocqueville has modified his definition of equality, as we saw reason to argue that he did in the *Souvenirs*; or whether he has simply fallen back into his old usage. My own view is that he is, unconsciously, trying to have it both ways: to use the old rhetoric to express new ideas. Both in the *Souvenirs* and in the *Ancien Régime* he grapples with the real problems and miseries confronting the peoples of Europe at the end of the old order; the abstract terminology of the *Démocratie*, with its mighty glimpses of the will of God and the march of equality through history, was not really suitable for the interpretation of such material. Yet all historians must make generalisations, and Tocqueville, of whom this was outstandingly true, fell naturally into his usual vocabulary when the need arose. He was not fully alert to the difference, discovered sooner or later by every historian, between making generalisations about the grand sweep of history and generalisations about economic conditions in Europe at a given date, or whatever other low, factual matter a writer is dealing in. What is surprising is how little this hurt his reasoning. His general picture is clear, coherent, and convincing. He talks of equality as the basis of the Revolution, when it was rather the battlecry of men hammering at the door of feudal privilege: the superstructure, not the foundation. This does not obscure his point that equality, in the eighteenth century, defined itself in terms of what it was *against* – the old order. The Third Estate would no longer endure the injustices and oppressions of the nobility. In the last resort, this is a class interpretation of the Revolution, not unlike Tocqueville's view that the 1848 Revolution was an assault by the masses on property, the last privilege of the classes.

Having settled to his own satisfaction the general nature of the Revolution, Tocqueville turns to the particular questions of why did the storm break in France rather than elsewhere? and what distinguished the Revolution in France from similar movements in other countries? They could scarcely be answered without a detailed picture of the workings of the Revolution outside France, in Germany, say, or Italy; and Tocqueville did not live to paint such a picture. Equally they could not be answered without a detailed picture of France, and to that the *Ancien*

Régime is devoted: hence the somewhat specialised character it bears in the memory of the reader.

Book Two is a portrait of the old order as it existed, in Tocqueville's view, about the time of Louis XV's death. Three main themes are emphasized: that it was an order formally founded on obsolete privilege, which impaired efficiency and equality every day; that it was equally characterised by administrative and political centralisation, another evil; that nevertheless a form and spirit of freedom still survived. The central preoccupations of Tocqueville's thought thus dominate the scene. The reader will inevitably wonder if they do not, perhaps, distort it.

It must be conceded at once that to some extent they do; but the striking thing about the *Ancien Régime* is the manner in which Tocqueville's luminous intelligence leads him on to original discoveries, while saving him on the whole from egregious errors such as are often committed by men wedded to theses. For instance, in the course of his work in the archives, where he toiled through vast numbers of administrative reports, Tocqueville not only began to sense that the Revolution was inevitable, an easy enough thing, if philosophically dangerous, to believe; he began to see that many of its most characteristic traits were already present, in force, well before 1789. This applied to his bugbear, administrative centralisation, of course, and perhaps it was the discovery of pre-Revolutionary centralisation which put him on the right track; but however he arrived at it, it was a true discovery. He makes the point with particular success when discussing the position of the peasants. They had become a class chiefly consisting of independent landowners long before 1789. There was a far more numerous independent peasantry in France than anywhere else in continental Europe. Consequently, although feudal dues and privileges had, in fact, eroded further in France than almost anywhere else, those that survived were the more resented. They were irritating checks on an almost complete freedom; vexing relics of a social inequality which was being eroded by economic facts. The exactions of the feudal lords were often real economic burdens on the peasant. Yet, though sanctioned by time and custom and rotten parchment bonds, they could no longer be justified by any social or military function performed by the nobles; nor did they reflect the distribution of political power within the system, for the noble was as powerless as the peasant.

This is a searching picture. No modern historian would accept it as a complete one, or as completely accurate: the system of privilege under the old order was more complex than Tocqueville allows, and here, as elsewhere, he underrates the vitality and power of the noble corps. But we must be careful above all to note Tocqueville's main concern, which at least will put his picture in its proper light. He is not saying that injustice, in the form of privilege, alone caused the Revolution; he does not even bother to show, though he clearly assumes, that the destruction of the remaining feudal burdens was one of the most important works of the Revolution. As one with his eye cocked at the nineteenth century, he wants to establish that the French peasant, with his hunger for land, his yearning for complete social and economic independence, and his hatred of privilege, had not changed in a hundred years. The importance of this concern to Tocqueville will become clear as we go on.

He is at the same game in the chapters describing centralisation. The very titles make the point: *How administrative centralisation is an institution of the old order, and not the work of the revolution or the Empire, as has been thought* (Bk. II, ch. 2); *How what today we call paternalism was an institution of the old order* (Bk. II, ch. 3); *How administrative justice and the legal immunity of public servants were institutions of the old order* (Bk II, ch. 4); and so on. Tocqueville has no difficulty in establishing, in overwhelming detail, the correspondence between the old order and the new. Thus, in chapter 6 (*Of administrative practices under the old order*) he lists what he takes to be, and assumes his readers will take to be, characteristics of the bureaucracy of his own day, and then shows that they existed under the old order too: the passion to see and supervise everything from Paris, which led to endless paperwork and delay; a governmental obsession with statistics; the closed-shop mentality of the bureaucrats, all alert to resent interference from outsiders; the special, flat, vague language of official documents; the dead hand of officialdom impeding economic progress; an instinct to control and censor the Press, though books were largely left alone, out of Philistine contempt (so he says, incorrectly – no doubt he was unconsciously led astray by the state of affairs under Napoleon III). Tocqueville does see and say that in some respects the old order differed from the nineteenth century France – for example, its rigid rules, he remarks, were laxly applied and repeatedly set aside, thus encouraging a certain contempt for the law; but he has no difficulty in showing that, if the Revolution was a centralising force, it was because the old order had implanted the instinct for centralisation in the breast of every Frenchman. All the Revolution needed to do was to re-establish the central government on stronger, sounder lines. He thus once again made it possible for himself to offer reflections about the old France which would apply to the new. Historically, this was a most dangerous, indeed absolutely misleading, process; and Tocqueville had still not clarified his pet concept, centralisation, sufficiently; but for the moment we need do no more than note again what he was about.

Talk of centralisation naturally leads him on to talk of the centre, of Paris. Here again his concern with his own times is obvious. He never mentions Versailles. His picture of the capital is far truer of Paris in the June Days than on the Quatorze Juillet, and is not even thoroughly true of the June Days. Tocqueville lays great stress on the pre-eminent position of Paris under the old order, and the extent to which the provinces looked for a lead to Paris; but he does not measure it against the hard facts of the revolutionary movement in the country at large (it is the mistake of the *Souvenirs* all over again). He alleges that Paris had already become a great manufacturing city before 1789, and that it was the labouring people thus concentrated in the capital by economic processes who brought down the old monarchy as they brought down Charles X and Louis Philippe, and as they tried to bring down the Second Republic. There is an important sense in which this picture is true, but it is not the sense in which Tocqueville meant it. He was not talking of the actual *sans-culottes*, who were chiefly artisans, but of industrial workers, such as he had seen in Birmingham and Manchester on his English visits, and such as he imagined (wrongly) to predominate in the Parisian crowd of 1848. Tocqueville ventured his bold generalisations simply because this was a subject on which he took it for granted that he was right: he read back what he took to be mid-nineteenth century conditions into the late eighteenth century without a qualm. He did the same a chapter or two further on, when he assumed that the marital exclusiveness of the nineteenth-century French nobility was characteristic of the old order: quite wrongly, for the pre-revolutionary noble never hesitated to marry money. Only his defeated descendants set a pre-eminent value on noble blood, their last, untouchable asset[1] (which explains the resistance of his relations to Tocqueville's own marriage).

Having established the existance of centralisation under the old order, at any rate to his own satisfaction (for the concept remains as ambiguous as ever) and that it was excessive (for he admits that France needed some degree of centralisation to survive) Tocqueville begins to discuss its evil effects, in revivalist pages reminiscent of those in the *Démocratie* which denounced the evil effects of equality. Perhaps unsurprisingly, the effects are much the same in both cases. The chief victim of centralisation is public spirit, that virtue which liberty so effectively fosters (thus he introduces the greatest of his *leitmotive* almost casually). Frenchmen had been levelled under the weight of the monarchy: among the educated classes, at least, intellectual and social tastes and traits had been largely homogenised; a nation of Frenchmen had been created out of a bundle of provincials (Tocqueville does not find it necessary to mention that provincial loyalties remained very strong). But this uniformity was not the same as unity. The classes hated each other, and clung to the privileges which separated them and protected their identities; they completely lost the habit of co-operating for the public good. Men became identified completely with the social grouping – nobility, *bourgeoisie*, peasant, worker – to which they belonged, and sank all other considerations in the immediate interest of that grouping. This phenomenon Tocqueville calls 'group individualism', a forerunner of that nineteenth century individualism which blinded a man to his duty and which

1. I owe this point to Miss C B A Behrens, who also remarks that Tocqueville once knew better: in an early essay on the old order he expressly discusses the frequency of marriages between poor nobles and the daughters of rich commoners. (See AR 42) This sort of inconsistency is not uncommon in his writings: he had the human weakness of sometimes forgetting what he knew.

Tocqueville had so earnestly deplored in *Démocratie II*. Yet (he adds, in what looks like an inspired guess) this system was so obviously crazy that even the members of the groups were ready to see its destruction, provided that what followed was an order without privilege. Equality, if it came, would be welcomed as a matter of common sense, and any attempt at restoring inequality would be fiercely resisted. And, in Tocqueville's opinion, equality had been sure to come, if only because this system of privilege was, in the end, a system of tax evasion which no modern state could afford. The monarchy had escaped from the competition of the Estates-General by selling privileges: in the end the contradictions and inefficiency involved brought it down, and the Estates-General had to be summoned again at last. Their convocation meant the death of privilege.

So far Tocqueville's picture of the old order has been one of almost unrelieved gloom: all the worst aspects of France under Napoleon III seem to have existed under Louis XV. But now we are to learn that this was not quite so. In some respects the old order was superior, a rebuke to Tocqueville's own slavish times. In the eighteenth century, he says, the spirit of Frenchmen was unbroken. The sale of offices made it impossible for the Crown to control its officials. Its power was of uncertain extent. The Kings were self-confident enough to be moderate – 'they never imagined that anyone would dream of dethroning them. They had none of that natural but cruel fear which has subsequently characterised so many governments.' (AR 169) The nobility had not lost the careless self-confidence conferred by centuries of leadership; they could resist oppression vigorously, and lead the demand for reform; they were high-spirited and free-spoken to their rulers. The clergy, enjoying entrenched privileges and great wealth, were similarly enlightened and able, and largely independent of State and Pope. Like the nobles and the Third Estate, they clung to their privileges, of course; but they were in the forefront of the demand for reform in 1789, and Tocqueville goes so far as to doubt that there had ever been a clergy more remarkable than that of France on the eve of the Revolution. The *bourgeoisie* had offices and immunities like those of the aristocracy, which bred in it a quasi-aristocratic independence of mind. The *parlements* were old and enfeebled, but (according to Tocqueville) they were still the judicial institutions of a free people, and as such frequently called the King to account. The culture of the eighteenth century was high-minded and disinterested – men had not yet been corrupted by modern materialism. The tradition of love between the Kings and the people meant that men felt they obeyed by choice rather than by compulsion. So France remained a free nation in spite of centralisation, and was thus able to undertake the work of '89, in which the spirit of freedom was so conspicuous; but because of the divorce between the spirit of freedom and the spirit of administration, the revolutionaries were ill-prepared by experience to replace the old order by a stable government and a healthy freedom under law.

Book Three of the *Ancien Régime* has a family resemblance to Book One of the *Souvenirs*, for both offer to explain the fall of a crown. But just as the great Revolution of 1789 was a more earthshaking affair than the February Revolution of 1848, so Tocqueville's analysis of its causes, brilliantly lucid though it is, is more complex, and harder to summarise, than his earlier essay. Fortunately Tocqueville himself gives his own summary in the last chapter of this book. France, he says, was the place where the general Revolution first erupted because there the feudal system survived shorn of all its good features, but keeping its bad. The nobility had ceased to lead or rule (this, by the way, was one of Tocqueville's more startling errors) but clung more and more closely to its unjust privileges. The monarchy had centralised the life of the country of Paris, and in so doing had made Paris potentially its own master and destroyer. Devoid of practical and theoretical knowledge of politics, the élite egged the people on to demand redress of grievances – unaware that this was playing with fire. There being no effective free institutions and no political parties, influence accrued to inexperienced writers, who propagated root-and-branch, impractical utopianism. (In an earlier chapter, Tocqueville was very hard on the writers, such as Voltaire and Diderot: 'virtue in a writer is often vice in a statesman, and the same things which often go to make up fine books can lead to great revolutions.' (AR 200) We may suspect, as sometimes before, an element of self-criticism here.) The French had learned to be passive before the monarchy, and were therefore ready to be passive before a revolution; and such a revolution could not be controlled. It could not be controlled by the élite who launched it, since they had long kept aloof from the masses, and did not know how to co-operate among themselves; it could not be controlled by the Church, for that was swept away with the established order with which it had identified itself; hence men's consciences were liberated for any evil (for Tocqueville believed, and, in the *Ancien Régime*, repeatedly stressed, that religious belief was necessary to keep the masses well-behaved). The Revolution was dominated by the people, conditioned as they were to savage violence by their life under the old order, and lusting as they were for revenge. They found the ideology propounded by the writers very convenient cant.

So the French Revolution acquired its popular, violent character with, according to Tocqueville, sad results. For what had started as the expression of twin passions for equality and liberty, tearing down in the names of these great principles absolutism and centralisation, became a chaos. Consequently men decided to abandon the dangerous joys of liberty : centralisation and absolutism were restored. Nothing, however, would induce them to abandon equality. Ever since, while the demand for liberty had been fitful, transient, and easily defeated (if never wholly crushed) the desire for equality had made steady advances and never retreated. Here Tocqueville is essentially reiterating a point made in his *Souvenirs*, where, it will be remembered, he argues that the Revolution of 1830 was primarily a last victory over the old order. 1830 confirmed that the system of privilege was dead for ever : equality had come to stay, though liberty was still to be won. Thus half the programme of 1789 had been achieved.

It would be possible to stop here, and coolly assess the merits and demerits of Tocqueville's presentation. But to do so would be to miss the point, and Tocqueville himself takes a different tack. His purpose in writing has been to understand the history of the sixty years following the fall of the old order (say, 1789–1848) and, as I have emphasized, to make sure that the right lessons are drawn. So now, in his last two pages, he explains that the Revolution cannot be understood entirely without reference to the character of the French themselves, independent of the causes he has listed and analysed at such length. Indeed he finds the nation more extraordinary than anything in

its history, for it is a tissue of contradictions. The French
are

> the most stay-at-home, the most routine-bound of men, left to
> themselves, but once uprooted, willy-nilly, from home and
> habits, they are ready to go anywhere and dare anything;
> disobedient by nature, they nevertheless adjust better to
> arbitrary and even violent rule by one man than to free and
> legal government by an élite; today the sworn enemies of all
> submission, tomorrow abandoning themselves to slavery with
> a passion that those nations best suited for servitude cannot
> match; led by a string when no-one has set the example of
> resistance, they are ungovernable as soon as that example
> appears; always deceiving their masters, who either fear them
> too much or not enough; never so free that tyrants may des-
> pair of enslaving them, never so enslaved that they cannot
> break the yoke. (AR 249)

(Napoleon III, take heed.) Only such a nation, so brilliant and
yet so rash, could have generated an event so extraordinary as
the Revolution.

This passage, the last in the book (save for a conditional
promise of another volume) raises several points, which must
be considered before I close the account. In the first place,
there can be no mystery as to why Tocqueville chose to end on
this note of impassioned rhetoric. Looking back over the *Ancien
Régime* as a whole, and remembering the purposes set out in
the Foreword, we can see that he attempted and achieved a
political portrait of the French in his time which might en-
courage liberals and (who knows?) discourage tyrants. Tocqueville was a member of two dispossessed élites: the élite of birth,
the nobility of the old order, and the élite of merit, the educated
gentlemen who had ruled France in the same name of liberty
and law from 1815 and, especially, from 1830, until the rise of
Louis Napoleon. He was too intelligent, and had experienced
too much, to take comfort from fantasy: political defeat can be
very enlightening. But he did want to see if there was good
ground for hoping that the liberal defeat might be as transient
as liberal victory. The passage on the French national character
shows what his conclusion was. Looking back at the rest of the
book, we can find other arguments: the independence of the

peasantry, those natural republicans, which Tocqueville traced back to the height of the old order; the libertarian traditions of the old French nobility; the universality of the Catholic religion which (Tocqueville thought) might well come to think that it flourished best under a democracy; the pride and greatness of the French as a nation. Of course there were factors working against all this, chiefly associated with centralisation and the two classes he most disliked, the *bourgeoisie* and the urban workers; but he might well feel that he had at least given sociological arguments sufficient to disturb the slumbers of the latest Bonaparte.

In the *Ancien Régime*, then, he had been writing of the eighteenth century while thinking of the nineteenth, just as, in his *Démocratie*, he had written of America while thinking of France. This had naturally led him into many serious historical errors – more than I have had space to indicate – but in justice to Tocqueville it must be added that he had given a new turn, not just to the study of the French Revolution, but to the study of history itself. If many of his assumptions about the scope and purpose of historical enquiry now seem trite, it is because everyone has copied him. Tocqueville, who was more conscientious than vain as an author, would not have cared much. The *Ancien Régime*, more even than his earlier books and speeches, proves to us how completely he was dominated by his passion for liberty, and by his will to convey that passion. It also contains his most explicit remarks on the subject, and thus enables us to attempt a final assessment of his work.

Liberty, he expressly tells us, is not just hatred of a tyrant, or even of tyranny. Nor can even a sceptical modern believe that Tocqueville was merely expressing or translating a class interest by his emphasis on this value. Liberty, for him, was a positive moral quality : the free man was measurably superior to the unfree. Above all, the chief benefits of liberty were not material :

It is very true that in the long run liberty always leads those who know how to keep it to comfort, well-being, often to riches : but there are times when it impedes the attainment of such goods; and other times when despotism alone can momentarily guarantee their enjoyment. Men who take up liberty for its material rewards, then, have never kept it for long. (AR 217)

What in all times [he goes on] has attracted some men so strongly to liberty has been itself alone, its own peculiar charm, independent of the benefits it brings; the pleasure of being able to speak, act, and breathe without constraint, under no other rule but that of God and law. Who seeks in liberty something other than itself is born to be a slave . . .

The taste for liberty, he concludes,

. . . wakes of itself in the noble hearts that God has created to receive it; it fills them, it inspires them. It is useless to try and convey it to mediocre souls who have never felt it. (AR 217)

This is the language of a moralist, an ideologist, a liberal. Tocqueville, with his stress on such qualities as self-respect, self-government, obedience to the law, respect for moral and intellectual superiors, has an ideal of the human personality and human society which may be called by many names. We can see in it a large inheritance from his own noble ancestry, aristocrats of the sword and the law; more than a trace of intellectual snobbery (we remember how he responded, in America, to the complaints of those who felt that the American voter was not enough impressed by learning); and we know that he pursued this ideal with an almost complete disregard of the trifling grievances, such as disease, starvation and unemployment, that preoccupied lesser mortals. None of this matters. Ultimately, ideology is not only a matter of conditioning, but also a matter of choice. There will no doubt be many who reject Tocqueville's creed either because it seems inappropriate to today's society, or because it seems inadequate or distasteful to them personally; or both. Equally there must still be many who, knowing Tocqueville's shortcomings, nevertheless believe, like him, that the flame of liberty cannot and should not ever be put out; who still see it as indispensable for the attainment of full human stature, whether to individuals or societies; and who are still grateful to Tocqueville for writing so intelligently, well and passionately in defence of their common goddess.

References and Booklist

All translations in this book were made by me, with the exception of the passage from Tocqueville's letter to his wife on p. 15 which is taken from *Tocqueville and Beaumont in America*, by G W Pierson, New York, 1938, p. 698.

Most citations are taken from the new edition of Tocqueville's works, which, under the direction of J P Mayer, has been appearing since 1951. Where it was necessary to use the obsolescent nineteenth century edition, prepared by Gustave de Beaumont, the fact has been clearly indicated. For the rest the system of reference used is as follows:

DA I   *De la Démocratie en Amérique*, volume I. Introduction par Harold J Laski. Note préliminaire par J-P Mayer. Gallimard, Paris, 1951; revised edition, 1960.

DA II   *De la Démocratie en Amérique*, volume II.

Souv.   *Souvenirs*. Texte établi, annoté et préfacé par Luc Monnier. Gallimard, Paris, 1964.

AR   *L'Ancien Régime et la Révolution*. Introduction par Georges Lefebvre. Gallimard, Paris, 1952.

The following are the most useful translations of Tocqueville's works:

Democracy in America. The Henry Reeve text as revised by Francis Bowen, now further corrected and edited with a historical essay, editorial notes, and bibliographies by Phillips Bradley. Vintage Books edition, New York, 1954.

Democracy in America. a new translation by George Lawrence. Edited by J P Mayer and Max Lerner. Fontana, London, 1968.

Recollections. A new translation by George Lawrence. Edited by J P Mayer and A P Kerr. Introduction by J P Mayer. Doubleday, New York, 1970.

The Ancien Régime and the French Revolution. Translated by Stuart Gilbert. Introduction by Hugh Brogan. Third Impression, Fontana, London, 1971.

Journey to America (Tocqueville's notebooks). Translated by George Lawrence. Edited by J P Mayer. Faber, London, 1959.

Journeys to England and Ireland (Tocqueville's notebooks). Translated by George Lawrence. Edited by J P Mayer. Faber, London, 1960.

The following works will be found of special interest to the Tocquevillean novice:

Drescher, Seymour. *Tocqueville and England.* Harvard, Cambridge, Mass., 1964.

Herr, Richard. *Tocqueville and the Old Regime.* Princeton, 1962.

Lively, Jack. *The Social and Political Thought of Alexis de Tocqueville.* Oxford, 1962.

Alexis de Tocqueville: Livre du centenaire. Centre National de la Recherche Scientifique, Paris, 1960.

Mayer, J P. *Alexis de Tocqueville.* Harpers, New York, 1960.

Pierson, George Wilson. *Tocqueville and Beaumont in America.* Oxford University Press, New York, 1938.

Redier, Antoine. *Comme disait Monsieur de Tocqueville ...* Perrin, Paris, 1925.

Senior, Nassau William. *Correspondence and Conversations of Alexis de Tocqueville.* Henry S King, London, 1872.